What Others Are Saying About
DEEP NATURE PLAY

"Joseph Cornell is a hero to many of us. His newest book is a beautiful meditation on and guide to achieving a state of awareness that he calls 'deep nature play.' This melding of nature connection, mindfulness, compassion and fun offers, no matter our age, creative passage to the worlds around us, to knowledge and to peace. In these times, we need deep nature play and Joseph's gifts more than ever."

—**Richard Louv,** author of *Last Child in the Woods*,
The Nature Principle, and *Vitamin N*

"Beautiful, profound, thought-provoking, deep, and true. *Deep Nature Play* is a wonderful book that takes us on a journey into the secrets of discovering nature by touching our very core, stirring our senses, and making us intensely joyous. Through the help of Joseph Cornell's books, I have experienced the great joy of communing on a deeper level with nature. In *Deep Nature Play*, he gently guides us to 'discover, through nature, our own higher nature.'"

—**Mahrukh Bulsara,** Co-Founder, Ecomantra
Nature Awareness and Travel, India

"No one is more effective than Joseph Cornell in connecting people of all ages with the profound peace, joy, and exhilaration available to us through direct experiences in nature. In *Deep Nature Play*, Joseph brings us an enchanting, authoritative, and important new guide for why and how to experience nature's gifts in our daily lives."

—**Cheryl Charles, PhD,** Co-Founder, President, and
CEO Emerita, Children & Nature Network

"*Deep Nature Play* reveals a direct pathway to our most authentic selves. During play, Joseph Cornell explains, we become completely absorbed in the present moment. Our creativity is unleashed and we become joyfully, wholly alive. This book is pure delight!"

—**Kathryn Gann,** Vice President, Theosophical Society in America

"Leave it to Joseph Cornell to give us the counterintuitive news that play is more important than ever: that for every animal, but especially human beings, it is a key to a happy and meaningful life. This book will bring joy into your world, if you let it!"

—**Bill McKibben,** author of *Radio Free Vermont*

"This book connects us to the joy of learning."

—**Joe Baust,** Former President, North American Association for Environmental Education, Emeritus Professor, Murray State University

"Every educator should read *Deep Nature Play*. And adults who want to reclaim their childlike openness and joyful connection with life will love this book. I was moved, inspired, and impressed."

—**Joseph Selbie,** author of *The Physics of God*

"Joseph Cornell offers oodles of practical tips and tools for playing more deeply and sharing this powerful teaching tool with others. *Deep Nature Play* is a fantastic new resource for teachers, parents, camp counselors, and grandparents."

—**Rocky Rohwedder, PhD,** Professor Emeritus, Environmental Studies and Planning, Sonoma State University

"I am amazed how well Joseph Cornell describes the benefits of deep nature play and the processes behind it. In our work, we use forest pedagogy to promote science among children and adults. His book gave me the inspiration and the challenge to transform forest pedagogy activities into Deep Play."

—**Urša Vilhar, PhD,** Slovenian Forestry Institute, co-author of *Handbook for Learning and Play in the Forest*

"*Deep Nature Play* is a guide for living joyfully and playfully while exploring our connection with nature. It shows how we can supercharge our brains and enhance our creativity, cognition, learning, memory, and brain plasticity. Cornell's book is a must read for anyone who wants to feel uplifted and connected to others and to nature. It will enhance your health, physically and mentally, and help you live your life to the fullest, with an expanded awareness of your own nature as joy."

—**Sue Mangala Loper-Powers** RN, MN, NP, C-IAYT, Former President of Washington State Nurses Association, Director of Ananda Yoga Therapy Training

"*Deep Nature Play* offers an essential message for all ages and cultures. So much love and depth of experience has gone into this book—it is clear Joseph Cornell has devoted his life to being deeply engaged in nature and is an awe-inspiring teacher."

—**Elizabeth Murray,** author, artist, gardener, and teacher

"Few people besides Joseph Cornell could have written *Deep Nature Play*. As he shares experiences from the participants in his nature awareness workshops, you begin to see the profound impact he has had on a number of generations. His inspiration and gentle ways of immersing people in nature are not just for children—I have seen adults of all ages and backgrounds completely absorbed and shedding tears of joy."

—**Alan Dyer, PhD,** Founder of the Centre for Sustainable Futures, Plymouth University, UK

"In *Deep Nature Play*, Joseph Cornell guides us to a deeper level of engagement with nature and with one another. He provides the rationale adults need to do what children know innately: having fun in nature fosters creativity and learning. Parents, educators, indeed anyone leading outdoor experiences, will find that the Flow Learning process and nature games enrich interactions with nature and engage people mentally, physically, and emotionally. This book is a perfect bridge for connecting adults with children, and us all with the joys of playing in nature."

—**Janet Carrier Ady, PhD,** Chief, Division of Education, Interpretation, and Partnerships, Bureau of Land Management

"As one of the earth's leading nature awareness educators, Joseph Cornell has brought a new and fresh look to the field of the natural world and its exploration. This exceptional work should be on every educator's go-to bookshelf."

—**Tom Mullin,** Associate Professor, Parks and Forest Resources, Unity College, Maine

"If you are a practitioner in the field of environmental awareness, or a person who feels the need to get outside and take an enlivened breath of fresh air, then this book is definitely for you!"

—**Jon Cree,** Trustee for the UK Forest School Association, environmental trainer and educator

About "Sharing Nature"

"The first edition of this book sparked a worldwide revolution in nature education and became a classic." —**National Association for Interpretation**

"This classic volume belongs on any short list of the most important environmental books." —**Bill Mckibben,** author of *Deep Economy,* founder 350.org

"I found *Sharing Nature with Children* a most original and imaginative concept in a field which is vital for the welfare of the planet."
—**Sir Peter Scott,** conservationist, a founder of World Wide Fund for Nature

"The games nurture children's tendency to regard the world with wonder, and they remind us, as adults, of ways to experience the joy and expansion of being one and at home with our Earth." —**Alexandra Dowd,** *One Earth* magazine

"A magical tool to awaken children to the delights of nature."
—**John Hodgson,** The National Trust, England

"Absolutely the best awareness of nature book I've ever seen. It has become justly famous because it works." —*Whole Earth Review*

About other Joseph Cornell books

"As a teacher, naturalist, and storyteller, I have used Joseph Cornell's Sharing Nature books as the core of much of my work. Now, with *The Sky and Earth Touched Me,* Joseph shows how to connect with nature on an even deeper level. This book is an instructional manual for all who wish to live in harmony with Planet Earth." —**Frank Helling,** U.S. National Park naturalist, educator

"*The Sky and Earth Touched Me* is a phenomenal book. After reading it from cover to cover, I intend to absorb its every nuance over the coming months and years. Cornell's book is going to be a Nature-Bible-Workbook for us here at University of the Living Tree, which we will use for inspiration and as a reference tool for workshops and courses. Profound and movingly written, it is presented with clarity and simplicity."
—**Roderic Knowles,** Founder of Living Tree Educational Foundation, Ireland, author of *Gospel of the Living Tree*

"*Listening to Nature* is a splendid masterpiece that captures the 'Oneness' we are all seeking to achieve with Nature." —**Tom Brown, Jr.,** author of *The Tracker*

DEEP
NATURE
PLAY

JOSEPH BHARAT CORNELL

DEEP
NATURE
PLAY

A Guide to WHOLENESS, ALIVENESS,
CREATIVITY, *and* INSPIRED LEARNING

CRYSTAL CLARITY PUBLISHERS
NEVADA CITY, CALIFORNIA

Crystal Clarity Publishers
Nevada City, CA 95959

Copyright © 2017 by Joseph Bharat Cornell
All rights reserved. Published 2018.

Printed in China

1 3 5 7 9 10 8 6 4 2

ISBN-13: 978-1-56589-322-1
ePub ISBN-13: 978-1-56589-575-1

Cover and interior designed by
Tejindra Scott Tully

[CIP data available]

Crystal Clarity Publishers
www.crystalclarity.com
clarity@crystalclarity.com
800.424.1055

*For the childlike spirit
within each of us.*

CONTENTS

FOREWORD
BY TAMARACK SONG

I used to be a classic example of what Joseph refers to in this book: a play-deprived adult plagued by "constant mental chatter," someone who thinks that games are solely for children. I was quite content to learn by "simply sitting and listening."

In his 2005 classic *Last Child in the Woods,* Richard Louv coined the phrase, *nature-deficit disorder,* to describe the current increase in developmental and behavioral issues—especially evident in children—that stem from insufficient time outdoors. Clearly, I suffered from this disorder—and that wasn't all.

Joseph describes eloquently in this book how play, and *deep play* in particular, enlivens one's whole being. Play heightens our sensory awareness, helps us feel alert, alive, and absorbed in the now. We operate at the peak of our mental and physical capacity. Because of my own lack of play in nature, I relegated myself to a cool, intellectual relationship with nature. Taking Richard Louv's phrase one step further, I would say I suffered from *play-deficit disorder.*

To help me out, unfortunately, I didn't have what you now have in your hands: the inspiration and guidance of Joseph Bharat Cornell. Intellectually, I had a basic awareness of much of what Joseph shares in this book: that play is a great learning tool that energizes us, fosters creativity, and helps build relationships. But I lacked the tools and processes to apply that awareness.

My salvation came from the same source as Joseph's inspiration for his life's work—nature herself. Joseph describes how a special moment with snow geese instilled in him the undying desire to immerse himself in nature. For me, it was wolves.

Through a series of serendipitous events, I became the caretaker of a pack of semi-domestic timber wolves. The wolves became my family; my marriage had gone sour, I was struggling with employees at work, and fed up with the state of the world. I began to feel closer to the wolves than to any of my own kind.

The wolves accepted me as I was. They saw through my dysfunction—and my stoic façade— and insisted that I be real with them. Through a combination of body language, bared teeth, and avoidance, they coaxed me out of my grumpiness and got me to . . . yes, *play*.

I am not referring to ordinary throw-a-stick-and-retrieve-it play, but rather, deep play. The wolves and I remained calm and stress-free, and therefore were able to absorb ourselves fully in the spirit of play. To join them, I had to cast aside my ego and personal agendas.

We played games of deception—and games akin to tag, hide-and-seek, and discover the hidden object. Playing was everything: we were completely consumed by it. When we made wrong moves and went tumbling head over heels, we'd pop back up and hardly miss a beat.

At the same time, the wolves could switch gears in a flash. Something very small, like a butterfly, a sudden breeze, or a strange sound might catch their attention. They would instantly stop and perk their ears. An aura of serenity would overtake them, and they would merge with their surroundings like fog drifting through the treetops.

The wolves' spontaneous responses to such moments remind me of Joseph's description in chapter 12 of the children's discoveries while playing the *Camouflage Trail* game. These are beautiful examples of what Joseph means by the singular focus of deep play, and its ability to concentrate the life force.

One day when I was out hunting meadow voles with the wolves, I jokingly admonished them: "Quit playing!" In that moment, it hit me that the hunt is a game. No wonder their life force was concentrated, and no wonder they gave their all—fun as it was, this was serious business! Games are training for the hunt, and the hunt is a game being played deeply.

Of course, we ask ourselves, "What's in it for me?" Very few of us have to hunt for our food, and our survival is not dependent upon whether we engage in deep nature play. However, there is something else for which we all yearn: I believe we long to feel fully awake, engaged, and operating at our highest potential. I believe we wish to feel a profound rapport with nature when we go there to play, and that we harbor a natural desire to express what Joseph calls "gratitude for the woodland's exquisite beauty." If this isn't reason enough for deep nature play, what would be?

Tamarack Song is the director of the Healing Nature Center and the Teaching Drum Outdoor School. His latest books are *Becoming Nature: Learning the Language of Wild Animals and Plants* and *Zen Rising: 366 Sage Stories to Enkindle Our Days.*

AN INTRODUCTORY STORY

I t was a brisk, clear day in Germany's Rhön Mountains; the magnificent beech forest surrounding us made a perfect setting for our outdoor program. The participants were playing *Silent Sharing Walk*, one of many Sharing Nature activities we enjoyed that day.

In *Silent Sharing Walk*, participants in teams of three stroll serenely through an area chosen for its natural beauty. When a walker is captivated by something, he or she gently taps the shoulder of other players, then points to the object. The players silently share the experience.

The German "sharing teams" walked slowly and silently under a canopy of stately beeches. The forest floor was populated with early spring wildflowers and a few small shrubs. I sensed among the members a tangible harmony with one another as well as with the forest.

The *Silent Sharing Walk* was not long: 120 feet. I stationed myself at the end of the trail to silently greet each finishing team. One German naturalist approached with twinkling eyes and a bright smile. He gestured for me to follow; I knew he had found something special. He led me back along the trail for perhaps fifty feet, then gestured toward the edge of the trail; he wanted *me* to find the magical surprise. I looked carefully over the ground before me; I saw blue wildflowers, a mossy rock, and forest litter, but I knew I should be seeking something unusual. Then it came into focus: a perfectly round nest, stitched together with spider silk—filled with four baby birds, their feathers just beginning to fill out. Superbly camouflaged, the nest and fledglings were all but invisible.

Most people would not have spotted the nest of birds. When absorbed in deep play, however, our sensory awareness is heightened; we become immersed in the present moment and feel intensely alert and alive. Because play is fun and rewarding, we operate at the peak of our mental and physical capacity.

How does deep nature play differ from regular play? Deep play has greater absorption with the object of play. It is a matter of degree—an important distinction for any parent, educator, or outdoor leader who wants to help others to *feel* a part of nature, or to truly understand any other field of study.

This book is for those who perhaps have forgotten how to play, or who wish to incorporate more play into their lives, and for educators who want to teach their subject matter with greater impact and inspiration. This book is also for parents and early childhood educators who desire to nourish and keep alive their children's innate curiosity and playful spirit. Most of all, this book is for those who want to touch and feel life deeply.

In 1979, I published my first book, *Sharing Nature with Children*. Soon after its release, there was a tremendous worldwide response to the book's playful games and uplifting message. Soon I began leading nature awareness programs throughout North America, Europe, Asia, and the South Pacific. The book quickly sparked a worldwide revolution in nature education and connected millions of children and adults with nature.

Why was there such an enthusiastic response to *Sharing Nature with Children* and its experiential games? The answer readers have given me over the decades is that they have, through practice of the book's principles, through nature play, felt in themselves joy, intense aliveness, and inner illumination. My sincere hope is that the present book will take you even deeper into the wonders and joy of nature.

Chapter One

PLAY
IS
UNIVERSAL

Animals love to play. "Mammals and birds of many species play by themselves, with others of their own species, and with members of other species." (Robert Fagen) Crows will slide on their backs on a steep snowy slope, then fly to the top to slide down again; bison will repeatedly sprint onto a frozen lake, then bellow gleefully as they skid across the ice. Brown bear cubs who play the most, Alaskan scientists have found, live the longest.

Why is play behavior so prevalent in the animal kingdom? Play surely has survival value; otherwise, why would mammals and birds expend precious energy playing? Through play, animals explore their world and discover all its possibilities. In higher animals, play stimulates the brain, enhances cognitive function and adaptability, and strengthens social bonds. Beyond these biological and social explanations, interestingly, scientists are starting to believe that play is a means by which animals can express their joy of life.

"The highest form of research, is essentially play." (N. V. Scarfe) Through his "thought experiments," Albert Einstein could visualize a concept and see the unseen. It was by this means that he discovered the theory of general relativity, which has been called the most influential theory in the history of modern science. "Imagination," Einstein once said, "is more important than knowledge," because knowledge tells us only what is known already whereas imagination tells us what can be. Play is imaginative; and play's openness, aliveness, and newness are essential to creativity.

Play is also immersive; it absorbs us in the object of our play. In the movie *Billy Elliot*, a poor Irish boy learns how to dance. When Billy is asked why he likes to dance, he replies, "I forget myself completely. I'm just there. Flying like a bird." Young children, Maria Montessori said, have an "absorbent mind," and they become immersed in their universe. Adults and adolescents can also, through deep play activity, re-experience a child's profound connection with the world.

In the early 1970s, as I studied to be an outdoor educator, I discovered how play energizes and enlivens people's experience of nature. Most of the outdoor learning at the time used the "walk—stop—talk" model: The leader stops at a subject of interest, talks to the group about it, then leads them to the next station. The approach was intellectual, with an emphasis on learning facts.

When I led people on nature walks, I wanted them to be totally engaged. I found that playful games would capture their attention and make learning multidimensional and fun. No longer were participants passively observing the environment with just their intellect; with play, their whole being became involved. Because participants were utilizing all of their faculties of perception and knowing, both children and adults came alive, and nature came alive for them.

Intrinsic to play are the following traits: curiosity; open-mindedness; high energy; eagerness to learn; and joy. If the goal of every nature outing is to enhance students' understanding of and relationship with the natural world, play can be a phenomenal ally.

As a young naturalist, I intuitively sensed the importance of play and began to design play-centered nature-awareness games. People would become so engrossed in the playful games that their game experience would lead them seamlessly into immersion in the natural world.

As I successfully used games as a teaching tool, I became aware that using the games in a certain sequence created a beautiful momentum toward a greater awareness of nature. From that realization came Flow Learning™—an outdoor teaching system that gently, almost magically, guides participants to uplifting nature experiences. (This learning system is discussed further in chapter 12.)

A growing number of people today see the importance of adding more play to their lives. In the following chapters the reader will discover the principles of deep play and its many gifts. A number of recent research studies have proven play's impressive benefits for both wild animals and human beings. To enhance the reader's understanding of play, I will share many of these fascinating discoveries.

Chapter Two

PLAY IS INNATE AND INTEGRAL TO LEARNING

Young children are like sponges: they absorb the world around them. Their innocence and their heightened attentiveness and awareness enable them to soak up experiences and information effortlessly.

In her book *Original Mind*, neuroscience pioneer Dee Joy Coulter, drawing on contemporary brain research, reports that "[m]ost children under the age of six live in a realm of direct experiencing, engaging the senses, and becoming absorbed in events as they occur without activating the constant mental chatter of the adult mind."[1]

In *Leaves of Grass*, the American poet Walt Whitman celebrated the remarkable aptitude of young children for absorptive learning:

> . . . a child went forth every day;
> And the first object he look'd upon, that object he became;
> And that object became part of him . . . .

A small child can be mesmerized by a butterfly in a field of flowers. For a brief moment, that butterfly can become the child's whole world. I can still vividly recall such an experience when I was a boy, playing alone outside on a cold foggy morning. Suddenly I heard a startling chorus of "whouks" coming toward me through the air. I peered intently at the thick fog, hoping for at least a glimpse of the geese. Seconds passed; the tempo of their cries increased. They were going to fly directly overhead! I could hear their wings slapping just yards above me. All of a sudden, a large flock of pearl-white snow geese burst through a gap in the fog. The sky seemed to have given birth to snow geese. For five or six wonderful seconds their sleek and graceful forms were visible; then they merged once again into the fog. Ever since this deeply thrilling moment, I have wanted to immerse myself in nature.

To know trees, John Muir maintained, one must be as free of care and time as the trees themselves. At the age of five, Richard St. Barbe Baker, the illustrious forester and conservationist, begged his nurse to allow him to walk alone in an English forest. Once alone in the forest, St. Barbe experienced what he called a "woodland re-birth":

> [A]t first I kept to a path which wound its way down into the valley; but soon I found myself in a dense part of the forest where the trees were taller and the path became lost in bracken beneath the pines. . . . [A]ll sense of time and space [was] lost. . . . I became intoxicated with the beauty around me, immersed in the joyousness . . . of feeling part of it all. . . . The overpowering beauty . . . entered my very being. At that moment my heart brimmed over with a sense of unspeakable thankfulness which has followed me through the years . . . .[2]

The elation St. Barbe Baker felt in the forest* was akin to "the 'state' athletes call the *Zone*, what researchers and professionals refer to as *Flow* and what children call *Play* [all of which] share selfless absorption and complete engagement in the moment."[3] (Michael Mendizza)

The elements of deep play are essential to an engrossing experience of nature. The attributes of deep play are: being fully in the moment;

---

* St. Barbe's passion for trees led him to Kenya in 1920 to begin his social forestry work: to encourage local people to reforest their land. Through his international organization, Men of the Trees, and other organizations he assisted, St. Barbe was responsible for planting billions of trees. Wherever St. Barbe traveled, people would suddenly decide to plant a few million trees. His rapport with nature enabled him to inspire countless thousands to re-green the earth.

experiencing a sense of timelessness; feeling deep rapport with the focus of play (e.g., elation at seeing geese emerge from the fog, gratitude for the woodland's exquisite beauty), and having a diminished consciousness of self. Learning requires keen attention. Self-forgetfulness and deep receptivity—hallmarks of deep play—enable us to apply our entire being to the task at hand.

Play is inner-directed and self-rewarding. Because the player's will and energy are completely committed—not divided by and preoccupied with external pressure or convention—the player experiences an exhilarating sense of wholeness.

Why don't our schools recognize the power of play in learning? The founder of the Living Wisdom Schools, Michael Deranja, a colleague and friend, once visited a public school class of kindergarteners, then afterwards, a class of high school students. The five-year-olds were full of joy and zest for learning. The teenagers, unfortunately, were bored and listless. Feeling compassionate concern at their indifference, Michael asked himself, "Where did their joy in learning go?"

In contrast, when Catarina, a twenty-year-old Finnish woman visited Ananda Village in California, she was asked, "How did you like going to school in Finland?" Catarina's face lit up with joy and she exclaimed, "I loved it! We had so much fun."

Finnish educators put a strong emphasis on play because they believe children learn best through play and self-discovery. Finland has been called the international all-star of education because its students consistently excel in academics. In a 2006 study of teenage students in fifty-seven countries, Finnish fifteen-year-olds ranked first in science, second in math, and third in reading. The emphasis on self-directed learning, collaboration, cooperation, and developing the whole person keeps Finnish students curious and engaged throughout their school years.

A spirit of play is intrinsic to every human being. Play—propelled by the player's own drive and enthusiasm—is, by its very nature, a perfect antidote to apathy.

Many older children and adults today are play-deprived; play could help them reconnect with their innate wonder and spontaneity.

Our motivation for play comes from within; from play comes inventiveness, joy, and connectedness with the focus of play that can keep us curious and creatively engaged throughout our adult lives.

Maria Montessori said that if you compare the learning ability of an adult with that of a child, you will find that an adult requires sixty years of hard work to match what a young child can learn in three. As people age the natural openness, confidence, and adaptability of their early childhood years generally subside, to be replaced by such inhibitors as self-criticism and fear, inhibitors that often stifle an adult's ability to learn. Two of the benefits of deep play—self-forgetfulness and living in the present—effectively quiet critical self-talk and other habits harmful to one's capacity to learn.

Chapter Three

A POSITIVE
LEARNING
EXPERIENCE
IS ESSENTIAL

During every outdoor session that I lead, my overriding goal is to inspire in others a loving rapport with the earth. One of Sharing Nature's tenets—*a sense of joy should permeate the experience*—ensures that participants develop an eagerness for learning about nature.

A growing relationship with the natural world—and a potential lifelong interest in nature—are far more important than knowing specific biological material. Conventional education often tries to cram factual information into the minds of students. Such an approach is shortsighted, for it values content learned over the welfare of the person learning.

Studies have shown that learning is "state-specific"—that the emotions experienced while learning something are retained along with the material learned. When someone revisits a previously learned subject, the same emotions experienced originally surface again. Michael Mendizza and Joseph Chilton Pearce elaborate on this phenomenon in their book, *Magical Parent Magical Child*:

> Imagine . . . a five-year-old boy learning to kick a soccer ball. Dad begins patiently by offering instruction on running, foot placement, ball alignment, spin, and velocity. Being less interested in performance than his well-meaning dad, the boy fails to reach . . . the "expected" skill levels.
>
> The boy would rather just play. . . . Dad [however] grows frustrated. His tone becomes focused, more intense. Sensing the tension, the boy's attention splits. Part of his attention goes into "trying" to kick the ball, the other part is channeled into defense. Performance plummets when [the] attention splits. Dad yells. The boy cries. On a good day perhaps 3 to 6 percent of dad's verbal instructions will be remembered. . . . [T]he disapproval and shame may last a lifetime.
>
> If learning 2 + 2 = 4 was fun, for example, subtle feelings of play or joy will be experienced along with the next challenge to solve an equation. If learning to spell or trying

out for Little League was humiliating, fear will be lurking in the background at the next spelling bee or athletic contest.[4]

In 1989 I was invited to Germany to address a large European symposium on nature education. The organizer of the event told me that over the past decade in Germany, educators had tried to impress on children the seriousness of Germany's environmental problems. They felt this knowledge would help children grow into adults who would make wise environmental choices. To their surprise, they discovered that on a national level, their students were turning away from nature. The symposium chair gave this explanation: "Learning all the problems of the environment had made thinking about nature so painful for the children that they lost their enthusiasm for environmental education."

I am happy to say that because of that symposium, with its hundreds of thoughtful educators open to the idea of making learning experiential and playful, nature education in Central Europe has become much more life-affirming and engaging. The children's natural love for the earth has been allowed to flower and grow strong, to create a firm base for caring for the planet.

"What I like about Sharing Nature," one outdoor educator told me, "is that children are learning and don't even know it." Children become so absorbed in the learning experience that they forget their negative associations with formal learning—boredom and perhaps coercion.

Sharing Nature games fire the imagination because they foster a living contact with nature. Annie Sullivan, the gifted teacher of the blind and deaf Helen Keller, gave young Helen almost all of her lessons outdoors. Helen later said that she "learned from life itself." When outdoor learning is experiential and touches the heart as well as the mind, children and adults become totally captivated.

Outdoor leaders should, like Annie Sullivan, create a learning environment that is experiential, safe, and loving. Such an environment will support true play, which is intuitively inspired, courageous, inventive, positive, and sees only possibilities and solutions. Play of this caliber revitalizes and uplifts the human spirit.

Chapter Four

PLAY ENERGIZES US

Nothing happens until something moves.

—Albert Einstein

Two years after the Berlin Wall was dismantled, I gave a workshop in the former East Germany. As I introduced Sharing Nature's methodology, twenty-five educators sat completely still, their frozen faces unreadable. The idea of experiential education was, I sensed, new to them. After living under an oppressive government for many years, they were cautious about expressing their thoughts and feelings.

But as soon as we began to play a lively nature game, one that demonstrated how to make learning fun, all twenty-five faces instantly lit up with joy. When we move physically, we become more alive, because movement in play lights up the brain.

I grew up in the 1950s along the Feather River in Northern California. When I was ten years old, I began running in the dark to greet the morning sun. With youthful exuberance and joy, I often ran through the shallow lakes and marshes. I loved how the awakening dawn enlivened the earth, with golden light flooding the fields and ponds.

Biologists have observed instances of solitary antelopes bounding playfully across the prairie, leaping and twisting their bodies vigorously. (Scientists believe that this extreme play movement mimics predator-avoidance behavior.) At the Grand Canyon, I've watched ravens spend hours playfully diving and soaring in the currents of air. In her book *Deep Play*, Diane Ackerman suggests that many animals find such a sense of effortlessness enjoyable. Certainly humans do—just watch skiers and surfers in motion.

MOVEMENT ANCHORS THOUGHT

People used to believe that thinking and movement were completely separate activities. Carla Hannaford, author of *Smart Moves: Why Learning Is Not All In Your Head*, saw a profound connection: "Learning, thought, creativity and intelligence are not processes of the brain alone, but of the whole body. . . . Memory is not stored [solely] in the brain [but in] neural pathways that fire together as patterns throughout the entire body."[5]

In the *Meet a Tree* game, a blindfolded player uses all his sensory faculties (except sight) to get to know a particular tree. Because the player experiences the tree through multiple faculties, it's usually easy for him to find his tree again. I have seen how children can—months later—walk unerringly to their special tree.

One day, in a stand of similar conifers, I observed an eleven-year-old girl walk tentatively up to a pine tree, reach out with her arms to encircle it, then close her eyes. After three seconds had passed, she opened her eyes and gave me a big smile: she had found "her" tree by comparing the tree's circumference to her body's memory of the original tree's circumference—a tree she'd met five months earlier.

"As children encounter new information, they will move to embody it on all their muscles and senses. . . . [Three-year-olds] actually move their bodies to conform to the physical configuration of [a] new object to better understand it."[6] Movement anchors thought and stimulates full body/mind integration. When we mimic, for example, the gait of a deer or a tree's life through the seasons, the movement deepens our understanding of the subject.

My friend Renata once played *Sounds*, a simple sensory awareness game, with her seventy-three-year-old Lithuanian grandmother, Mary, who has Alzheimer's disease. Since the onset of Alzheimer's, Mary has been always anxious and restless; it's been difficult to find any activity—even walking in nature—that can calm her anxiety.

During one visit, Renata took Mary into the backyard garden. Renata asked Mary to close her eyes and listen to the sounds around her. "Grandma," she asked, "can you raise a finger for each sound you hear?"

For eight minutes, Grandma listened attentively to the sounds around her, raising her fingers at each different sound. Then, opening her eyes, she began carefully listing each sound she'd heard: a bird, a car, people talking, the wind in the leaves, her granddaughter breathing, and an insect flying by.

After just a few minutes of playing the *Sounds* game, to Renata's amazement, Mary was transformed. She had become calm and focused, and her face was shining with joy. For nearly an hour afterwards, Mary's calmness remained.

Recent studies show that the physical senses are closely connected to memory and cognition. "As we grow older, we get more forgetful and distracted in large part because our brain does not process what we hear, see, and feel as well as it once did."[7] (Brain HQ) Because play requires focus and total involvement, and activates multiple centers of perception and cognition across the whole brain, it supercharges learning and memory.

Scientists used to think that the human brain stops growing after the young adult years. Researchers have now discovered, however, that the brain can change at any age, a phenomenon called *brain plasticity*. In addition to plasticity in which neural pathways are created and changed by our actions and our thoughts, the brain can actually produce new neurons in adults who are physically active. Play can keep us young in spirit, no matter our age.

Some adults feel that sensory awareness games are solely for children. I've been amused to see how parents, at the beginning of family programs, will gently push their children toward me, then themselves stand at the back, their arms folded across their chests. When I tell the parents that I need them to partner with their children to play a game, they are more than eager to help. Immediately, the adults are playing just as enthusiastically as the children. All of us, no matter our age, can benefit from joyful, living contact with the earth. Playful nature games help teens and adults experience life with a child's natural exuberance, and reconnect us with the innocence and joy of our own childhoods.

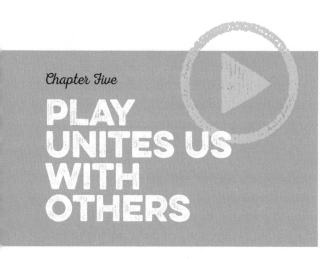

Chapter Five

PLAY UNITES US WITH OTHERS

D o animals play fair? Prominent field biologist Marc Bekoff believes they do.[*] Because play is rewarding and joyful for social animals, they have a built-in incentive to keep play going.

Among mammals, play often involves simulated biting and fighting. To avoid nonaggressive play being misinterpreted as real aggression, Bekoff explains, "Dogs and other canids [such as foxes and wolves] use specific play signals to initiate and to maintain social play. . . . [They] use a bow to tell one another such messages as 'I want to play,' 'This is still play no matter what I am going to do to you,' and 'This is still play regardless of what I just did to you.'" "And bowing is repeated during play . . . to insure that play doesn't slip into something else, like fighting or mating. After each individual agrees to play, there are ongoing, rapid, and subtle exchanges of information so that their cooperative agreement can be fine-tuned and negotiated on the run, so that the activity remains playful."[8]

---

[*] In *The Emotional Lives of Animals*, Mark Bekoff writes, "Dogs don't tolerate . . . cheaters, who may be avoided or chased away from play groups. . . . While studying dog play on a beach in San Diego, California, . . Alexandra Horowitz observed a dog she called Up-ears enter into a play group and interrupt the play of two other dogs, Blackie and Roxy. Up-ears was chased out of the group, and when she returned, Blackie and Roxy stopped playing and looked off toward a distant sound. In a fooling behavior, Roxy began moving in the direction of the sound, and Up-ears ran off following their line of sight. Having gotten rid of Up-ears, Roxy and Blackie immediately began playing again." Marc Bekoff, Ph.D., *The Emotional Lives of Animals* (Novato, CA: New World Library, 2007), 101.

Coyote pups "while . . . having fun . . . learn ground rules that are acceptable to others—how hard they can bite, how roughly they can interact—and how to resolve conflicts. There is a premium on playing fairly and trusting others to do so as well."[9] Dogs and their wild relatives use play to foster among pack members a spirit of fairness, trust, empathy, and cooperation—all qualities essential to harmonious group interaction.

When wild animals observe man's presence nearby, they usually stop playing because play requires total focus, and they cannot risk being caught unaware. Play among humans also subsides if we feel threatened, for our attention is then diverted from playing to protecting ourselves.

A hallmark of play is diminished consciousness of self. Over-competiveness and self-aggrandizing behavior make players *more* conscious of their egoic selves. For real play to thrive, it is imperative that its climate be positive and cooperative.

Play often requires that one focus intently to master a specific skill; many of Sharing Nature's activities challenge players, whether individually or in small groups, to accomplish a particular task. Genial competition is wholesome when it energizes and brings out the highest in everyone and when the players take delight in one another's success.

Play is a great equalizer. Among wild animals, differences in physical size and social rank are tolerated more during play than in other social settings. One can observe this same phenomenon when fathers wrestle with their children. Fathers typically use self-handicapping and role-reversal behavior to make the contest fair and fun for their children, who then play with confidence and vigor.

In his book *A Wolf Called Romeo*, Nick Jans tells the story of a wild wolf who for six years lived on the edge of suburban Juneau, Alaska; Romeo made friends with the locals and with their dogs. The adult wolf craved company and enjoyed playing with many of the local dogs. Being much larger than they, the wolf used role-reversal and self-handicapping to make his play with his potential playmates successful:

Most dogs matched Romeo's affable nature with their own.... If a dog turned aggressive, the wolf, instead of bowling over the offender, would tuck his tail and dodge it with a weightless burst or sudden leap and blend his moves into a game. We all became accustomed to the incongruous spectacle of a ...120-pound wolf striking appeasing postures before some mongrel that scarcely came up to his knees, and engaging in submissive play with rude underlings that he could have thrashed in an instant.[10]

Play makes us feel intensely alive. We are at our best when we play, and the resulting joy we feel is highly contagious. As we relate with others on play's loftier levels, shared elation strengthens group cohesion.

On the German-Polish border in the mid-1990s, I gave a three-hour workshop for a lively and diverse group: forty German teenagers, twenty-five German educators, and seventeen mentally challenged Scottish teenagers. Because the program was in the former East Germany, few of the Germans spoke English; none of the Scots spoke German.

I began the session with playful games to awaken everyone's enthusiasm and to make learning joyful. It was heartwarming to observe small groups of Germans and Scots communicating with one another despite differences in language, age, and intellectual ability. I could see growing in the group a beautiful rapport and family feeling.

To increase the group's receptivity, we played calming sensory-awareness activities; then, for a direct experience of nature, we played the *Journey to the Heart of Nature* exercise, in which each person discovers a special place in nature. The Germans and Scots were so focused on and absorbed in the natural setting, and in the experiential exercises, that it felt as if we were in a group meditation. It was moving to observe the group's closeness with nature and with one another.

Activities such as *Interview with Nature* unite us with the natural world. In this game, players look for a special rock, plant, or animal that has an interesting story to tell. For example, a player might choose a dragonfly, a yellow flower, a boulder, or even the wind. They then imagine what its life might be like, and ask their subject questions such as these: "What is it like to live here? Who comes to visit you? Is there something you would like to tell me?"

It's touching to observe players sitting quietly with their interview subject, contemplating its life and discovering that in its own way it is just as alive as they are.

Because the players are participating in a shared purpose as they solve challenges and experience nature in novel ways, Sharing Nature activities inspire not only a profound rapport with nature but also create a joyful camaraderie and cohesiveness among the participants.

Chapter Six

PLAY
ACTIVATES
THE WHOLE
PERSON

Johann, a professional German forester, described to me a profound change of attitude toward his work: "I was trained in my profession to see trees as a commercial commodity. But now, after experiencing the Sharing Nature activities, I realize that the grasses are my friends, the trees are my friends, that every living thing in the woodland is my friend. This, for me, is a new way of looking at trees. This awareness is going to fundamentally change the way I work with the forest."

As a participant in a Sharing Nature workshop, Johann interacted with trees in a variety of innovative ways. First, he and his co-participants, foresters from all over Germany, built a tree together. Several foresters acted out each tree part—tap root, lateral roots, sapwood, cambium, phloem, and bark—and in doing so experienced the nature and function of that tree part kinesthetically.

Johann was then guided through a visualization of himself as a deciduous tree, living through the seasons of the year. During the guided imagery, Johann planted himself firmly in the earth, spread his branches out, drew nourishment from the sun and sky, and turned air and light into life. With his sheltering branches, Johann cooled the summer air and warmed the winter air, thus making a more favorable environment for other life forms. Reenacting a tree's life enabled him to *experience* personally the role trees play in the forest ecosystem and to *feel* in himself many of the noble qualities of trees. By imagining himself living as a tree and nurturing the nearby plants and animals, Johann strengthened his sense of stewardship and love for the earth.

Earlier in the workshop, Johann, blindfolded, had "met a tree"; through his sense of touch, smell, and hearing, he explored the tree's unique features. Johann was then asked to remove his blindfold and—guided by what he remembered about his tree and the path leading to it—to find his tree again.

Johann also interviewed a venerable tree: "What events have you seen in your life?" Trying to feel the tree's response to this question, he looked for signs that could tell him how wind, high water, snow, fire, or an animal might have shaped the tree. He reflected on the many dramatic and commonplace events the tree had witnessed during its centuries of life.

The day closed with a song accompanied by graceful arm movements, an exercise that allowed Johann and his fellow foresters to celebrate their kinship with the forest and all living things.

The variety of learning modes enhanced Johann's imagination, intuition, reason, empathy, and love, as well as his kinesthetic and sensory awareness, and thus enriched his appreciation and understanding of trees. Sharing Nature exercises activate multiple centers of perception and cognition; they stimulate different parts of the brain and strengthen the neural connections between brain regions, thereby enhancing understanding, long-term memory, and creativity.

Just as different parts of the brain communicate with one another, trees communicate and share nutrients with other trees through what scientists call the "wood wide web," an underground fungal network connecting roots of trees in a forest. Contemporary botanists see a remarkable prescience in words spoken by the *Avatar* movie's fictional character Dr. Grace Augustine:[*] "What we think we know—is that there's some kind of electrochemical communication between the roots of the trees. Like the synapses between neurons."

A recent study by forest ecologist Suzanne Simard and her graduate students shows that Douglas fir and paper birch trees shuttle carbon seasonally back and forth to one another. During the shady summer months, the birch trees pass carbon to the sun-starved Douglas fir seedlings. And during autumn—after the deciduous paper birches lose their leaves—the fir seedlings, now receiving more sunlight, send carbon back to the birch trees.

When the fungal web is intact, plant diversity and the viability of a woodland community are significantly greater. Foresters in Germany have discovered that spacing trees artificially far apart to allow them to get more sunlight and grow faster, prevents them from establishing a viable fungal network and thereby lessens their resilience.

Similarly, when certain neural pathways in the human brain are never connected, or die off from disuse, one's ability to function in

[*] Although the movie was set in the year 2154, it was released in 2009.

ways associated with those brain pathways is diminished. The Swedish Pediatrics Institute found, for example, that children with little imagination, when confronted with an unpleasant, demeaning, or threatening situation, would lash out; they were simply unable to imagine an alternative response. Children with a strong sense of imagination, on the other hand, were far less prone to violence, because they could create an alternative inner scenario and thus respond harmoniously.

Simard's research found that large, older trees act as "Mother Trees," ones which transmit through the fungal web resources and biochemical signals to young tree seedlings as well as to other plants. In similar fashion, every flowering human faculty (and quality) nurtures and contributes to our sense of wholeness and integration. We are physical, mental, feeling, and spiritual beings; our learning and life activities should address and nurture our whole nature. Because of its multifaceted character, play can enhance many valuable human qualities: openness, curiosity, wholeheartedness, self-confidence, attentiveness, self-control, calmness, imaginativeness, and optimism.

Every field of study has its own principles and practical content that are essential for students to know. The more the learning process engages the whole person, however, the more interested, creatively inspired, and personally transformed the student will be. In environments where children, adolescents, or adults typically learn while simply sitting and listening, a sprinkling of carefully planned play activities can:

- Revitalize students by changing the style and pace of learning;
- Reinforce and deepen understanding of class topics;
- Act as a catalyst for future exploration.

"Nature must be experienced through feeling," said legendary naturalist Alexander von Humboldt. It is through the heart that we understand new and profound truths. If you want to motivate people, first touch their hearts, because it is their feelings that will inspire their thoughts and behavior.

In the words of the Japanese politician and social activist Tanaka Shozo (considered his country's first conservationist), the "care of rivers is not a question of rivers, but of the human heart." If learning is mainly mental, one's viewpoint on the subject tends to be materialistic. As a trained, practicing forester, Johann understood tree science well; but, alas, his scientific training had caused him (in his own words) to see trees simply as "a commodity."

Playful, multifaceted exercises enriched Johann's whole being. As he experienced the forest in a more living, nuanced way, Johann himself became a more empathetic human being.

Chapter Seven

CREATIVITY IS THE HEART OF PLAY

A child building a sandcastle; a scientist doing research in the laboratory; a painter experimenting with color—all use imagination to visualize a new creation. "Creativity," it is said, "is intelligence having fun."

It is also the innate human drive to improve upon life. A spirit of creativity provides the ability and self-confidence to navigate currents proactively. A creative person shapes—rather than being shaped by—outer circumstances. We each have head, heart, and two hands; how well we use them depends on our ability to transcend everyday thinking and its accompanying limitations—and to create new realities and possibilities.

Creative minds typically see many solutions to a problem. Stuart Brown tells of a biologist who trained river otters "to swim through a hoop by offering a food reward for completing the task. Shortly after the otters learned to do this, the animals started introducing their own twists to the task. They swam through the hoop backward and waited to see if they got a reward. They swam through and then turned around and swam back through the other way. They swam halfway through and stopped. After each variation, they waited expectantly to see if this version of the task would earn a reward . . . ."[11]

The otters, instead of repeating the original behavior that brought them the reward, experimented with different strategies in order to understand better the rules governing the game. Most adults, when confronted by a problem, refer to past experience for what has worked before, then try to solve the problem by the same means. The downside of looking to the past is that one becomes a creature of habit, applying tired solutions to new situations.

Studies show that 98 percent of three- to five-year-olds think divergently, while only 2 percent of adults do. Play encourages divergent ("outside the box") thinking; it generates a flurry of imaginative ideas; it provides a healthy corrective to the tendency to approach life in a fixed manner.

Play is a conscious discipline: "To play," according to psychologist Peter Gray, "is to behave in accordance with self-chosen rules. . . . Play draws and fascinates the player precisely because it is structured by rules the player herself or himself has invented or accepted." The result is that players have a greater commitment to follow the rules. Compliance with the rules requires mental effort and self-control. To maintain one's role while playing house or acting as a superhero, for example, entails subjugating one's "immediate biological needs, emotions, and whims."[12] When you're a superhero and happen to skin your knee, you can't cry!

Generally children behave without thinking about their behavior. Russian psychologist Lev Vygotsky discovered that "[w]hat passes unnoticed by the child in real life becomes a rule of behavior in play."[13] "In play, a child is always . . . above his daily behavior."[14]

Vygotsky spoke of two sisters, ages seven and five, who—like most siblings—sometimes played together, sometimes ignored each other, and sometimes fought with each other. When the sisters decided to *play* at being sisters, however, they began to dress alike, talk alike, and walk with their arms around each other. *Playing* sisters caused the girls to reflect on what sisterhood meant to them, on how sisters would behave toward one another. By acting in accordance with their idealized image of sisterhood, their interactions with one another became more intentional. *Playing* sisters, rather than *being* sisters, transformed their relationship: Such is the power of play.[15]

Each Sharing Nature activity enhances and elevates our relationship with the natural world. In the *Tree Imagery* exercise, for example, participants act as a tree, sheltering and nourishing forest life in its myriad forms. Because trees cooperate with one another more than they compete, they are often described as communal. Both trees and human beings dramatically influence their environment. In the case of humans, unfortunately, the influence isn't always beneficial. As *Tree Imagery* players adopt the role of a tree and offer sustenance to the life around them, they find themselves expressing a spirit of selfless giving. As players feel the energy of life flowing through their bodies, they experience a marvelous sense of vitality, resilience, and wholeness.

Just as the young Russian girls became better sisters by *playing* sisters, so can we become better members of Earth's great family by intentional play that enhances our relationship with our fellow beings.

The simple phrase "let's pretend" opens new vistas of creative insight. These magical words give us permission and freedom to suspend rationality—to think outside the box. Players of Sharing Nature's *Interview with Nature* pretend that everything in nature is alive and conscious; as they interview such natural elements as a tree, a bird, or a rock, they write down the responses they sense.

When I introduced *Interview with Nature* during a workshop in the New Forest in Southern England, I saw a warden with the Royal Society for the Protection of Birds looking at me skeptically. Nonetheless he decided to give the activity a try (even if the idea of conversing with a tree seemed peculiar to him); upon his return, he announced enthusiastically, "I had the loveliest conversation with a warbler!"

The thought "I am alive, and everything else *is* too" radically changes our experience of life. When we recognize that we share a universal aliveness, we feel united with the rest of creation.

The essential quality of creativity is the human drive to improve upon life. In nature play we can experience the highest part of ourselves, and discover the life that is improved upon—even transformed—is our own.

Chapter Eight

ATTUNEMENT: THE SECRET OF CREATIVITY

s a way to understand the difference between rational thinking and creative thinking, try the following experiment:

What do you see in the white space below?

●

Repeat your answer by saying it out loud.

According to Dr. Mike Bechtle, most adults reply: "A dot." When asked, "Is there anything else?" they'll respond: "A black dot." After doing this exercise 300 times with corporate audiences, Bechtle gave his summation: "I always get the same answer: 'It's a dot.' But a few times, I've had a chance to do the same thing with a group of early elementary school kids. When I ask what I drew, they've never once said it was a dot." Their responses were fresh and original:

"It's a squashed bug with no legs."
"It's the top of a telephone pole."
"It's a hole in a golf course."
"It's a black moon in a white sky."[16]

Every day we receive billions of sensory sensations, of which only a few grab our attention; the rest are stored in subconscious memory. Because the developed prefrontal cortex labels incoming sensations (this is a pebble, that is a chair), adults see life less directly—instead, it is filtered through their assumptions and preconceptions. Children, on the other hand, having fewer preconceptions, are more open to and enriched by the innumerable sensory stimuli flooding their being.

In her book *Original Mind,* neuroscientist Dee Joy Coulter tells of meeting a young Tibetan monk who demonstrated his ability to view the world without preconception: The monk turned his head and gazed at an imaginary object, then said, "I look.... I see a flower. First time." A few minutes later, the monk again turned his head, gazed across the room at the same imaginary object, and repeated, "I look.... I see a flower. First time."[17] For the young monk, it *was* possible to perceive the world clearly, without the hindrance of foreknowledge.

For most adults, said Coulter, "a second glance at a flower registers automatically as the same flower."[18] Deep play can help us see the world with fresh eyes. Especially effective to this end is *Camera,* one of the most popular Sharing Nature games—and one which offers players powerful moments of pure awareness.

The game is played with two people: one person is the photographer and the other the camera. The photographer silently guides the camera, whose eyes are closed, on a search for captivating pictures. The photographer, seeing something appealing, points the camera to frame the object. The photographer then taps the shoulder of the camera as a signal for the camera's eyes to open. Three seconds later the shoulder is tapped again, and the camera's eyes close. This three-second "exposure" has the impact of surprise and intensity: many players remember their photographs for five or more years, a testament to the acute focus the "camera" brings to the photos.

The one-pointed focus of *Camera* quiets the mind, thereby allowing the mind to act as a mirror, like a calm mountain lake reflecting a blue sky. Players of *Camera* receive into their consciousness the world around them.

During deep play, as you realize you have, in a very real sense, *become* a tree or an animal, the distinction between you and that tree or animal can disappear altogether. Rita Mendonça, Brazil's Sharing Nature national coordinator, once gave a training program in the Amazon for professional ecotourism guides, some of whom had worked in that area for forty years. Their attitude at first was that Rita (coming from the city of São Paulo) had little to teach them. But one woman, after participating in several Sharing Nature exercises, approached Rita and said with deep emotion, "You are helping me find the forest inside of me! We don't know the forest in this way!"

Reason can only describe a tree; it cannot help us experience the tree in its totality. By intuition, or calm feeling, we perceive life directly. Because timelessness and a diminished sense of self are characteristic of deep play, the players' emotional state is typically calm and stress-free—players are able to enter fully into the heart of their play.

Many celebrated inventors, artists, writers, and Nobel Prize-winning scientists credit their discoveries and creations to an ability to get inside their subject—through such means as play-acting and physical movement, careful observation, empathy with their subject, and especially imagination. "I never made one of my discoveries through the process of rational thinking," said Einstein. "Knowledge is limited. Imagination circles the world."

True understanding, philosopher Henri Bergson said, comes by "transport[ing] oneself to the interior of an object" to discover its "ineffable quality." Nobel laureate Barbara McClintock revolutionized the field of molecular biology by placing herself *inside* the corn genes and chromosomes she studied while viewing them under a microscope. She attributed her pioneering discoveries to "having a feeling for the organism":

> The more I worked with them the bigger and bigger [they] got, and when I was really working with them I wasn't outside,.. I was part of the system. . . . and everything got big. I . . . was able to see the internal parts of the chromosomes. . . . It surprised me because I actually felt as if I were right down there and these were my friends.[19]

"Before painting a bamboo," said Su Tung-P'o, "you must make it grow inside you." In Sharing Nature's *I Am the Mountain* exercise, the clouds, the hills, all nature become vividly alive. The player observes a beautiful part of nature, such as a stately oak, and then tries to feel the oak's essence inwardly—its spreading canopy, its swaying branches. The goal is to feel a living communion with the tree.

Becoming one with something "other" is the secret of creativity. Profound moments of rapport—with a deer, a flower, or a flock of sandpipers—inspire us to discover, and explore, new and enthralling worlds.

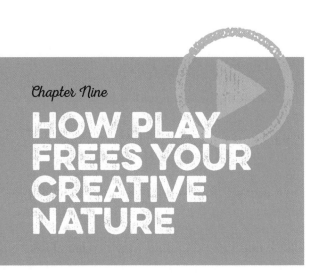

Chapter Nine

HOW PLAY
FREES YOUR
CREATIVE
NATURE

child's brain is designed to *learn*; an adult's brain is designed to *perform*. A self-critical focus on performance can lead adults to self-censor themselves: "Is my performance good enough?"

People spend much of their time conversing with themselves. We generally speak to ourselves ten to twenty times faster than we can speak out loud. Psychologists estimate that the average person entertains 1,300 self-talk thoughts a minute. Because the mind sees in pictures, it can grasp a thought in a nanosecond (one billionth of a second). For most people, the majority of self-talk thoughts (60 to 85 percent) are negative.

Self-consciousness is the greatest inhibitor to creativity. How can we discover anything new if we are recycling past thoughts—and perhaps insecurities—over and over in our minds? For creativity to flower, it must grow free of old patterns of thinking and being.

Children are uninhibited and naturally spontaneous; in their enthusiasm, they jump feet first into whatever they're doing. Through creative play, adults and adolescents can reclaim their innate spontaneity. If self-preoccupation is the death knell of creativity, play's accompanying self-forgetfulness is its rebirth.

Restlessness, too, blocks creativity. A recent Microsoft Corporation study measured how fast people's attention span has been dwindling. In the year 2000, the average Canadian's attention span was timed at twelve seconds; thirteen years later it was timed at eight seconds—a 33 percent decline. Today, even humble goldfish have a longer attention span than the average Canadian: nine seconds for a goldfish vs. eight for a Canadian.

I once demonstrated the prevalence of restlessness to a group of twenty-five teachers in Canberra, Australia. I asked them to look at a beautiful tree as long as they were able to, and to raise their hands when their attention wandered from the tree and drifted to other thoughts. By the six-second mark, every hand had been raised. The teachers were amazed at how restless their minds were.

In chapter 7 we learned that one key to creativity is becoming one with something "other." To deeply enjoy and resonate with a winter marsh or with a kaleidoscope of migrating butterflies, one's attention must be fully present. A sage once said that people use only 5 percent of their concentration; if we accept this statement as fact, people's experience of nature is only a twentieth of what is humanly possible.

Picture your thoughts as restless winds that ripple a lake's surface. Those winds prevent you from seeing in the lake a clear reflection of the trees and surrounding mountains. As the breezes die down, as your mind becomes more still, you will see the image of trees and mountains reflected more and more perfectly in the lake.

In 2010 two Harvard researchers, Matthew A. Killingsworth and Daniel T. Gilbert, discovered that adults think about something other than what they're doing 47 percent of the time.[20] Games that heighten the physical senses can curtail the mind's tendency to wander and thus bring us more fully into the present. One such Sharing Nature activity is *How Close?*, inspired by Enos Mills' epic journey traveling alone and completely snow-blind through the Rocky Mountain wilderness.

While walking outdoors, children and adults often pay little attention to their environment. Players of *How Close?* experience in a dramatic way the importance of being aware of their surroundings. A blindfolded walker—accompanied by an unobtrusive guide—uses the senses of touch, hearing, and smell to discover environmental clues in order to navigate safely across an open field or meadow, to walk in a straight line toward the leader.

When sight, our dominant sense, is removed, our other senses are heightened. Players of *How Close?* become especially attentive to the direction of the wind, the slope of the land, the location of the sun, microclimates, pungent smells, and the calls of birds and other natural sounds. The snow-blinded Enos Mills, during his three-day journey, was so attuned to his other senses that he could sometimes decipher the topography by shouting and listening to the returning echoes.

The qualities of deep play—self-forgetfulness, total immersion, timelessness, rapport and oneness with the focus of play—are also attributes of meditation. In deep stillness and expanded consciousness, the meditator can experience a flood of creative inspirations.

The following exercise will help you experience nature more deeply:

STILLNESS MEDITATION

When you practice this simple meditation in natural settings, your subsequent memories of those places will be vivid and strong. This technique quiets restless thoughts and brings a wonderful calmness. By repeating the word "stillness," the practitioner gently calms his thoughts and enters the present moment.

First, relax the body. Do so by inhaling and tensing the muscles of the whole body: feet, legs, hands, arms, back, chest, neck, and face. Then throw the breath out and relax completely. Repeat this practice a few times. Then take several deep, calming breaths.

From then on, observe the *natural* flow of your breath. (Do not control the breath in any way. Simply notice its movement.) Each time you inhale, think "still." Each time you exhale, think "ness." Repeating "still . . . ness" with each complete breath focuses the mind and prevents your attention from wandering away from the present moment.

As you are practicing the "still . . . ness" breath, calmly observe the landscape before you. If thoughts of the past or future distract you, calmly and gently bring your attention back to the scene before you, and continue repeating "still . . . ness" with your breathing.

⁕

This technique can help you enjoy beautiful wild areas longer and with more depth. Use Stillness Meditation, with eyes open or closed, indoors or outdoors, whenever you want to feel calm.

Chapter Ten

MINDFUL
PLAY

"Everything [in the wilderness] was so alive and familiar," said John Muir. "The very stones seem talkative."[21] While in the wilds of Tibet, British explorer Sir Francis Younghusband found that he "had a curious sense of being literally in love with the world. . . . I felt as if I could hardly contain myself for the love which was bursting within me."[22]

From my earliest years, I have often sensed a loving presence that permeates this world. One day while hiking through a remote valley in Desolation Wilderness, I felt an overwhelming sense of joy—a joy so pervasive that it seemed to animate the flowers, the stones, and the cascading stream. Every blade of grass, every tiny waterfall and mossy rock, seemed to radiate and rejoice in this all-encompassing joy.

I sat beside a small, snow-fed tarn, encircled by huge granite blocks cleaved by a glacier, delighting in the joy around me. Soon, a robust, cheery little bird (an American dipper) came within a few yards of me and began singing. His clear, melodious voice echoed superbly against the surrounding rock walls. The bird's vibrant song and its resounding echo greatly amplified the joy I felt that day on the mountain.

Nature's greatest gift, I believe, is in making us aware of the oneness of life. Nature cares for us in countless ways: she gives us sustenance, shelter, all our daily needs. Her most precious gift is the experience of her deeper nature: her stillness, harmony, wholeness, and joyful vitality. Since the early 1970s, as a university student majoring in nature awareness, I've wanted to help people discover through nature their own higher nature.

A teacher in the Southwest once asked the children in his class to draw a picture of themselves. He recalled, "The American children completely covered the paper with a drawing of their bodies, but my Navajo students drew themselves differently. They made their bodies much smaller and included in the picture the nearby mountains, canyon walls, and dry desert washes. To the Navajo, the environment is as much a part of who they are as are their own arms and legs."

The understanding that we are a part of something larger than ourselves radically reshapes our thinking and behavior. "What man takes in by contemplation," said Meister Eckhart, "he pours out in love."

David Blanchette is a teacher at the Punahou School on Oahu Island, Hawaii. There, every year he leads thirteen-year-old students on a nature excursion along a remote and wild coastline where they play the Sharing Nature exercise *Expanding Circles*. In this exercise, players find a place with a panoramic view and an interesting foreground. Then, in gradual stages, they expand their awareness starting from close by all the way out to the distant horizon, feeling themselves moving and becoming alive in everything they see. Below are representative comments made by his students after practicing *Expanding Circles*:

- I felt euphoria.

- I felt like I was one with everything around me.

- I was a calm ocean wave gently rolling towards the shore. I was the reef, feeling the cool water roll over me. Every part of me was moving and flowing in harmony.

After finishing the exercise, Jessica, one of David's students, wishing to express her appreciation for the ocean, gratefully wrote "thank you" in the sand, then let the waves wash her words away, as though the ocean were absorbing her gratitude into its vastness.

In addition to the exercises featured in this book, another of the author's books, *The Sky and Earth Touched Me*, contains many of Sharing Nature's most inspiring and powerful exercises. *The Sky and Earth Touched Me* guidebook is an effective resource for anyone seeking a deeper connection with nature.

Chapter Eleven

PLAY IS FOR EVERYONE

As a young professor, the Nobel Prize-winning physicist Richard Feynman rediscovered the benefits of one of play's core properties: apparent purposelessness, or play for its own sake. His discovery came at low ebb in his time teaching physics at Cornell University; he had become, as he puts it, "a little disgusted with physics." In his autobiographical *Surely You're Joking, Mr. Feynman,* he tells the story of his personal transformation: "I used to *enjoy* doing physics. Why did I enjoy it? I used to *play* with it. I used to do whatever I felt like doing—it didn't have to do with whether it was important for the development of nuclear physics, but whether it was interesting and amusing for me to play with.

". . . Now that I am burned out . . . I'll never accomplish anything, . . . [J]ust like I read the *Arabian Nights* for pleasure, I'm going to *play* with physics, whenever I want to, without worrying about any importance whatsoever.

"Within a week I was in the cafeteria and some guy, fooling around, throws a plate in the air. As the plate went up in the air I saw it wobble, and I noticed the red medallion of Cornell on the plate going around. It was pretty obvious to me that the medallion went around faster than the wobbling.

"I had nothing to do, so I start to figure out the motion of the rotating plate. I discover that when the angle is very slight, the medallion rotates twice as fast as the wobble rate—two to one. . . . Then I

67

thought, 'Is there some way I can see...by looking at the forces or the dynamics, why it's two to one?'

"...I ultimately worked out what the motion of the mass particles is, and how all the accelerations balance to make it come out two to one.

"I still remember going to Hans Bethe and saying, 'Hey, Hans! I noticed something interesting. Here the plate goes around so, and the reason it's two to one is...' and I showed him the accelerations.

He says, 'Feynman, that's pretty interesting, but what's the importance of it? Why are you doing it?'

"'Hah!' I say. 'There's no importance whatsoever. I'm just doing it for the fun of it.' His reaction didn't discourage me; I had made up my mind I was going to enjoy physics and do whatever I liked.

"I went on to work out equations of wobbles. Then I thought about how electron orbits start to move in relativity. Then there's the Dirac Equation in electrodynamics. And then quantum electrodynamics. And before I knew it (it was a very short time) I was "playing"—working, really—with the same old problem that I loved so much....

"It was like uncorking a bottle: Everything flowed out effortlessly....There was no importance to what I was doing, but ultimately there was. The diagrams and the whole business that I got the Nobel Prize for came from that piddling around with the wobbling plate."[23]

Like Feynman, people learn best when learning grows out of play. Because play is intuitive and inventive, players enter a creative flow in which new discoveries often come unsought. Play is joyous. To play is to love what we do; when we love what we do, we excel at what we do. The more rapport we feel with a subject, the more revelatory our experience and insight.

Feynman, like many adults, may have been performing routine tasks at work—jobs he could easily do automatically. Performing tasks that require only habitual, half-hearted effort leads to mental stagnation and boredom. Underused, one's inner being withers; apathy and disgust set in. The way back to healthy enthusiasm lies, as we see in Feynman's experience, in the fun and innovative nature of creative play.

The indifference displayed by many students in school and by many employees in the workplace is due in part to the lack of a spirit of creative play: the opportunity to be adventurous and original.

Michael Michalko, author of *Cracking Creativity: The Secrets of Creative Genius,* succinctly explains the limitations of logical thinking in this way: "usual thinking is logical and goal-oriented. Creativity is difficult with this kind of thinking because the conclusion is implicit in the premises." Logic can only perceive what is already known; it "leads us to the usual ideas and not to original ones. If you always think the way you've always thought, you'll always get what you've always got."[24]

Play's imaginative, adventurous spirit, on the other hand, can lead us to new peaks of inspiration and discovery, to heights where the inner being flourishes.

Stuart Brown defined play as "an absorbing, apparently purposeless activity that provides enjoyment and a suspension of self-consciousness and sense of time."[25] Being free of care is especially essential for one wishing to experience nature: "When you see the extraordinary beauty of the earth, its rivers, lakes, mountains . . . . the very majesty of the mountain makes you forget yourself. . . . you don't exist, only that grandeur exists." (J. Krishnamurti)

Children's native innocence and openness enable them to become one with the focus of their play. PGA Tour Champion Peter Jacobsen discovered, while keeping score for his ten-year-old son's basketball team, how totally absorbed children could be. At the end of the first half, his son's team had scored fifteen baskets, the opponents two. As his son's team ran back to their bench, they asked eagerly, "Mr. Jacobson, what's the score?" When he replied, "Well, it's thirty to four," the children, with equal enthusiasm, then asked, "Who's winning?" It may have been obvious to the coaches and parents who was winning, but for the children, the score meant nothing. They were playing. The only reason the children kept score was for the satisfaction of the parents and coaches.[26]

A University of Michigan study in the 1970s found that offering preschoolers a reward for performing a pleasurable activity instilled in them the idea that the activity was work rather than play. One group of children (three- and four-year-olds)—all of whom had enjoyed drawing—were told beforehand that they would earn an attractive "good-player" certificate for their drawings. The drawings of the *expected-reward* group, who now apparently viewed drawing as a task that one does for a reward rather than for enjoyment, were significantly inferior to those of the two control groups. The *expected-reward* group put only enough time and effort into their drawing to earn their reward.

Unlike the preschoolers in the other control groups, who kept on drawing spontaneously afterwards for the simple pleasure of it, the *expected-reward* group stopped drawing much earlier. They spent only half as long drawing spontaneously for the fun of it as did the other groups.[27]

When we are motivated by the thought of future reward rather than by the inner satisfaction that comes with performing the task itself, we, like the *expected-reward* preschoolers, lose our sense of delight in the moment.

Deep play thrives in the living moment. The disparity between thinking about the past or the future and living in the present is the difference between dipping one's toes in a pond and swimming in the ocean. Play immerses us in life itself.

Playfully swimming in the great ocean of life, swimmers feel their spirit soar—that all their actions are expressions of a joyful flow. Our friend "Parisa" described such an experience of exhilarating play and how it radically transformed her outlook, bringing her both outward success and inward fulfillment.

Growing up in Persia (now Iran), Parisa had a special love for her country's beauty. She married and moved to Canada; some years later she began taking courses for an advanced degree in biochemistry. While preparing for her PhD oral exam, Parisa studied intensely, memorizing thousands of facts.

When her husband asked her to join him on a business trip to the Canadian Rockies, she at first resisted, not wanting to interrupt her study, but finally agreed to go. Her husband attended his meetings; Parisa, absorbed in her studies, never left the hotel room.

After the conference was over, Parisa's husband convinced her to take a break from studying and spend some time walking in the mountains. As she reached a low-lying ridge, Parisa beheld the crest of the Canadian Rockies, a sight that reminded her of her childhood summers climbing joyfully in the mountains of Persia.

Running like a mountain goat, she scaled a nearby summit. She gazed at the vast range of peaks before her, and felt an overwhelming sense of stillness—a profound oneness with the towering mountains and blue sky. In that moment of exaltation Parisa realized that her exams meant nothing to her. Her joy in connectedness was all that mattered.

The experience of inner connection stayed with Parisa even after returning home. She felt relaxed and happy during her oral exams. Easily answering every question fired at her by the examining committee, Parisa successfully passed the exam and received her degree.

In her uplifted state, Parisa's consciousness had shifted from the tense mental grind of a graduate student cramming for exams to the peacefully absorbed and joyful state of a child at play.

"Life is only available in the present moment." (THICH NHAT HANH) Parisa's experience of deep play took her into the living present—and transformed her life.

Chapter Twelve

CONVERTING PLAY INTO DEEP PLAY

Hall of Fame golfer Johnny Miller was renowned in the 1970s for his brilliant golf play. During his unparalleled winning streak, he hit the ball consistently closer to the flag than had any player in history. "When I won at Tucson by nine shots," he said, "the average iron shot I hit ... was no more than two feet off line."[28] Playing felt like "golfing nirvana." Miller describes how magical it was to play golf at such a high level:

> In 1970 when I went out to win the Phoenix Open, it was like I was playing by myself. I had zero anxiety. No tension. No stress. I was completely confident. When I was over the ball I felt like I was weightless. I had a feeling that I almost could just float off the ground. It was a feeling of confidence but also a warm feeling inside that I was in control. I could dictate my own energy and paint my own picture out on the course. I was able to address every situation and find a creative answer. The shot would talk to me. I'd say fine.
>
> It was so much fun I couldn't wait to hit the next shot. I was taking every shot to the highest level . . . . Most golfers are only in the zone for a round or two in their life. . . . I did all my homework, but I'd listen to the child in me. I listened to that inner voice.[29]

In deep play there is no egoism, no personal agenda, no self-induced anxiety, tension, or stress; Miller's freedom from self-consciousness allowed him to become *one* with his golf play.

Deep play stimulates *authenticity*: acting from one's core, from a place of truth. While playing in the Phoenix Open, Miller felt a wondrous sense of energy, alertness, strength, clear thinking, and confidence. As his mind receded during play, the power of his soul shone through.

Play is a state of mind. Play's openness, limitlessness, connectedness, positivity, and harmony express our highest human qualities. To receive the full benefit of play, focus your attention wholly on the play activity. Let nothing else exist. In the following passage, John

Muir praises the experience of the total concentration of a mountain climber:

> In climbing where the danger is great, all attention has to be given the ground step by step, leaving nothing for beauty by the way. But this care, so keenly and narrowly concentrated, is not without advantages. One is thoroughly aroused. Compared with the alertness of the senses [at such times], one may be said to sleep all the rest of the year.[30]

The freedom from self-consciousness that attends immersive play can be healing. Stacy Bare was a U.S. soldier who served in Iraq. After his return to the United States, "he struggled with a host of problems: alcoholism, a cocaine habit, and suicidal thoughts . . . .'If I hadn't started climbing,'" Bare explained, "'I'd probably be another sad statistic. The focus it gave me let me leave my troubles on the ground.'"[31]

Like rays of sunlight illuminating a stained glass window, the focus required for wilderness pursuits intensifies the awareness, clears the mind, and sharpens the senses. When the spirit is uplifted, everything in nature—the beech leaves, the trills of forest birds—appears to glow with a pristine radiance.

Yoga science tells us that higher states of awareness depend on centering the life force within. The singular focus of deep play, like that of yoga, concentrates the life force and thereby enhances our experience of nature. As life energy gathers and flows in a single direction, we live life more abundantly.

Many years ago I had a dream that captured the elation that comes from rising above everyday experience:

> As I was riding a bicycle on a country road bordered on both sides by wheat fields, a large falcon swooped out of the sky and began flying right beside me.
>
> I looked at the falcon and the falcon looked at me—and then smiled. The falcon had a magical presence. When it began flying faster, I pedaled harder to keep up with this magnificent bird.

The falcon smiled again, this time seeming to ask, "Can you go faster?" By pedaling furiously, I was barely able to keep up with its faster pace. It took everything I had to stay even with the falcon.

Seeing that I was still keeping up with him, the falcon dramatically increased his speed. To my surprise, I felt a force propelling me forward, and I was able to stay abreast of the rapidly flying falcon.

I was being carried along by the falcon's presence.

Then the bird flew upward into the sky, and I found myself rising skyward with my falcon friend.

THE
FLOW LEARNING™
PROCESS

Flow Learning is a teaching system that creates an accelerating flow of inspiration. During its four-step process, players and play become harmoniously united.

Just as, during my nighttime slumber, I felt exhilaration in the flying falcon and became at home with him in the sky, Flow Learning, by creating a sequence of playful activities through cumulative stages, elevates play to deep play, and in doing so removes human barriers that separate us from the natural world. Flow Learning is not only a teaching method; it's a practice that brings us to higher understanding.

How much we bring play into work, school, or leisure time ranges from not at all to in every moment—the more we live playfully, the greater our joy and creativity. Because they are committing their whole being to the class topic, Flow Learning participants can experience greater purpose, focus, openness, and depth of understanding: all ingredients essential for true learning.

To change matter from solid to liquid, or from liquid to gas, requires energy; without energy, nothing will ever change or move. Energy is

also required to move a classroom of students. In this case, the energy comes from within the students themselves, generated by their will-power and spirit. By awakening their whole being, Flow Learning and the playful Sharing Nature activities generate in students a strong flow of intense interest in the subject. Because the full cooperation of their will is engaged, students are able to experience new vistas of learning.

Although originally I created Flow Learning for teaching outdoor nature classes, the same sequence can be used to teach any subject matter, whether indoors or outdoors. Flow Learning is based on the universal principles behind how people learn, become more aware, and mature as human beings. Tens of thousands of educators and outdoor leaders have found this teaching system extremely effective.

By choosing the appropriate games, you can meet people where they are, then guide them gently, step-by-step, to higher learning and play experiences. Flow Learning's four cumulative stages are: 1) Awaken Enthusiasm, 2) Focus Attention, 3) Offer Direct Experience, and 4) Share Inspiration. Each Sharing Nature activity is categorized by its appropriate stage. *Camera*, for example, is an Offer Direct Experience activity.

The Four Stages of **FLOW LEARNING**

This first stage stimulates eager and intense interest and enjoyment. The maxim "Any dead fish can float downstream, but it takes a *live* fish to swim upstream" humorously captures the need to be fully *alert* and *energetic*. Playing with others helps awaken just this state of mind—alert and energetic. Simultaneously, group play acts to free us from the personal distractions that are so stifling to our direct experience of life. And this direct experience is the true purpose of deep play. Awaken Enthusiasm games make learning instructive, experiential, and fun—and establish a rapport between teacher and student, student and student, and both teacher and student with the subject.

For example, in the Stage One activity *Natural Processes,* players act out a natural phenomenon such as the solar system or glaciation. During one workshop, a class of sixty divided into four smaller groups. Each smaller group took a turn acting its choice, with the other three groups as the audience.

One group gathered on an Alaskan beach to act out ocean tides. Holding hands, the players formed the shape of a crescent moon. From the crescent moon configuration, the players expanded out and around to simulate a full moon. Leaning backwards to represent radiating rays of light, they beamed bright illumination on the audience.

The group then quickly formed a line and walked up the beach to enact the incoming high tide. One player, acting the part of a barnacle, crouched ahead of the undulating "wave" and let the rising tide pass over it. The filter-feeding barnacle, previously dormant, then came to life, extending and waving its net-like feeding legs, or cirri. When the tide receded—enacted by the players walking backwards toward the ocean—the barnacle, left high and dry, withdrew its cirri and became inactive again.

To be nature-aware requires living in the now. How could it be otherwise? To see a tree demands that we truly *see* the tree. Go outdoors and practice the following exercise:

> Find a natural area that feels especially captivating, such as a small stream lined with maple trees, a flowery meadow, or an aspen forest. Gaze around you and enjoy everything you see and hear. Notice how, when you're deeply attentive, everything becomes vibrantly alive. Then observe how when your thoughts are distracted, the world of nature disappears. Continue observing the flow of your awareness, noting when you're fully present and when you're not.
>
> Imagine the power of sustained, engaged awareness. Only by focusing our attention completely can we meet nature face-to-face and truly know her.

Studies have shown that those who have had a spiritual awakening outdoors have usually been alone, and in a state of heightened openness. Deep play is essentially a personal, internalized experience, even if one is with other people. Focus Attention games pave the way for uplifting experiences by increasing our receptivity.

Every Stage Two game has a built-in challenge that requires focusing through one or more of the senses. In the children's game *Camouflage Trail*, hard-to-see objects (such as a large, rusted nail or a wooden clothespin) are placed along a section of trail. Players then walk the trail and try to spot as many of the objects as they can. One teacher, forgetting to mark the end of her *Camouflage Trail*, noticed that her students were so absorbed that they walked well past the finish line; carefully scrutinizing every patch of ground, the students were still looking for more objects.

During summer mornings, Henry David Thoreau often sat in his cabin's doorway from sunrise to noon, rapt in reverie, amidst the pines and hickories, in undisturbed solitude. He had a magical relationship with the animals living near his Walden Pond home.

Thoreau once told his visiting friend Frederick L. H. Willis, "Keep very still and I will show you my family." He began to make a low, curious whistle, which immediately brought a woodchuck running up to him. Then he whistled another low, distinctive note, and several birds, including two crows, flew toward him, one landing on his shoulder. After hand-feeding the animals, Thoreau dismissed each in turn with its own special whistle.

Being a habitual walker and a keen observer, Thoreau knew more about the natural and human history of the nearby farmlands than the farmers themselves. Most of all, Thoreau prized an intuitive experience of nature—non-rational, direct, and immersive. Thoreau called such experiences Beautiful Knowledge.

The activities in Flow Learning's Third Stage let nature be the teacher. Players surrender themselves to nature and embrace the wildness around them.

One popular Stage Three activity is *Vertical Poem*. To play, observe something that captivates you—perhaps a field of flowers or a secluded sea cove. Notice its effect on you, and choose a word that captures your feeling. Then use each letter of the word to begin a line of your poem.

In Taiwan I once led eighty people down a steep, narrow track to a stunningly beautiful gorge. The trail and chasm were so confining that I couldn't gather the group together. Vertical Poem was the perfect exercise for that setting. In the depths of the gorge, eighty people, immersed in the chasm scenery, composed vertical poems. Composing the poems quieted the group and allowed people to become more present, more immersed in their surroundings.

After climbing out of the canyon, many participants read their poems to the group—each poem beautifully and uniquely expressing our shared experience of the gorge.

STAGE FOUR: SHARE INSPIRATION

The purpose of Stage Four is to reflect on one's experience and to share it with others. Research has shown that simply having an experience is only a first step. Reflecting on the experience clarifies and strengthens its meaning. Using the arts—such as creative writing, storytelling, poetry, and drawing—to capture and express one's experience not only leads to deep play and introspective understanding, it also expands that experience through sharing with others.

Sharing brings to the surface one's individual inspiration in a way that can benefit everyone. Sharing also creates an uplifting atmosphere, one which reinforces and enhances group ideals and makes it easier for leaders to share inspiring stories and principles when people are most receptive to hearing them.

Ending a Flow Learning session with a song or story creates closure, fosters group unity, and inspires heartfelt rapport with the natural world.

Flow Learning is a practical and highly effective teaching process for any educator. You can read in-depth about Flow Learning and the many Sharing Nature activities in the author's book, *Sharing Nature: Nature Awareness Activities for All Ages.*

FLOW LEARNING

1 AWAKEN ENTHUSIASM

Quality: **PLAYFULNESS AND ALERTNESS**

- Builds on people's love of play.
- Creates an atmosphere of enthusiasm.
- A dynamic beginning gets everyone saying, "Yes, I like this!"
- Develops alertness and overcomes passivity.
- Creates involvement.
- Minimizes discipline problems.
- Develops rapport between participants, leader, and subject.
- Fosters positive group bonding.
- Provides direction and structure.
- Prepares for later, more sensitive activities.

2 FOCUS ATTENTION

Quality: **RECEPTIVITY**

- Increases attention span and concentration.
- Deepens awareness by focusing attention.
- Positively channels enthusiasm generated in Stage One.
- Develops observational skills.
- Calms the mind.
- Develops receptivity for more sensitive nature experiences.

CHART

Sharing Nature®
WORLDWIDE

3 OFFER DIRECT EXPERIENCES

Quality: **COMMUNING WITH NATURE**

- Fosters deeper learning and intuitive understanding.
- Inspires wonder, empathy, and love.
- Promotes personal revelation and artistic inspiration.
- Awakens an enduring connection with some part of nature.
- Conveys a sense of wholeness and harmony.

4 SHARE INSPIRATION

Quality: **CLARITY AND IDEALISM**

- Clarifies and strengthens personal experience.
- Increases learning.
- Builds on uplifted mood.
- Promotes positive peer reinforcement.
- Fosters group bonding.
- Encourages idealism and altruistic behavior.
- Provides feedback for the leader.

From *Sharing Nature: Nature Awareness Activities for All Ages*
Copyright © 2015 Joseph Bharat Cornell

The Joy of Flow Learning

"The Flow Learning strategy is so potent, so gentle, that it feels like the most natural and obvious way to communicate nature education to children and adults of any age. It works in harmony with people's innate states of being, channeling their energy and contemplation at the most effective times for learning and appreciating.

"One of my favorite aspects of Flow Learning is watching a group of strangers become physically and mentally attuned to one another and to their natural environment within minutes of beginning the first stage of the program, when the Flow Learning strategy's purpose is to awaken enthusiasm. Nervousness and shyness melt away as children and adults alike adopt a playground playfulness, and the group unites in a childlike spirit of innocence, inclusivity, and fun. They are now so open and willing to learn.

"What never ceases to amaze me is that people so easily engage with Joseph's activities, and that amongst the older children in particular you can see them excited at being encouraged to play and learn and explore their senses in a way that is too often restricted to only the youngest of children. At heart, I believe people of all ages truly appreciate opportunities to return to the simplicity of the young child's world, and the Sharing Nature activities and games allow and encourage us all to do that. An unspoken permission is granted, the weight of our years is removed by the opportunity to refresh and revitalize our spirit through playing with and within our natural environment."

—*Kate Akers*, *National Executive Member,*
New Zealand Association for Environmental Education

Chapter Thirteen

HOW YOU CAN PLAY MORE DEEPLY

"Children have all the fun," said an old man as he observed a toddler walking on a busy street, mesmerized by the parade of passing flowers, stones, and friendly people.[32] All people—no matter their age—have the potential to be captivated by life's everyday occurrences. Children's natural openness enables them to live in a world filled with enchantment—not because they're children necessarily—but because they live close to their inner being.

Peter Matthiessen in *The Snow Leopard*, recalls his young son's absorption in wild nature:

> In his first summers . . . my son would stand rapt for near an hour in his sandbox in the orchard, as doves and redwings came and went on the warm wind, the leaves dancing, the clouds flying . . . . The child was not observing; he was at rest in the very center of the universe, a part of things . . . . Ecstasy is identity with all existence . . . . [T]here was no "self" to separate him from the bird or flower.[33]

Matthiessen said that his son Alex, by the end of early childhood, had lost his rapport with the "wildness of the world." In her book, *Explorers of the Infinite*, Maria Coffey explains how young children lose their sense of connectedness after accumulating more life experience:

At birth, a child's brain has approximately 100 billion neurons. As the child grows, the number of neurons remains the same, but the connections between them, the synapses, along which neurotransmitters travel, develop as each new experience is cross-checked against previous ones. Gradually, a unique configuration of neuronal connections personalizes the brain, allowing the child to interpret the world in the light of previous experience. It is these thought processes and associations, built on accumulated experience and memory, that [British neuroscientist, Susan] Greenfield claims constitute the "self."[34]

Since small children have accumulated relatively few experiences, it is easier for them to go into the state in which they experience the world on a sensory level, without interpretation. As we age, however, this sense of wonder . . . become[s] stunted.[35]

Alex lost what all people lose: childhood's innocence and openness to pure sensory perception. Childhood's clear awareness is an innate gift, bestowed—not by a pristine brain—but by the human spirit. How can we as adults reunite with our true, authentic self? The answer lies in the self-integrating process of play.

Recent scientific studies have shown that contact with nature increases the feeling of aliveness, awe, and connectedness, and reminds us of life's higher priorities. During a workshop I gave in North Carolina, a Duke University student, feeling overwhelmed by her upcoming final exams, practiced *I Can See*, a simple Sharing Nature activity designed to help children become aware of their natural surroundings.

The activity is played with an adult sitting or standing behind the child. The adult begins by saying, *I can see*. The child then names the first thing he sees: for example, *the tall trees*. The adult continues prompting the child by repeating other simple phrases. After each one, the child replies by naming his experience:

Adult: *I can hear . . .*

Child: *the tap tap of a woodpecker.*

Adult: *I can smell . . .*

Child: *the flowering bush.*

Adult: *I can feel . . .*

Child: *the peace of the forest.*

Even though *I Can See* is played for just a few minutes, its facility for direct experience can bring children into the present moment. After we had played this activity for only three minutes, the Duke student, her face wreathed in smiles, described her transformation: "I immediately became aware of the world around me; I *saw* the nearby trees, I *heard* many forest sounds. I forgot about my exams and didn't feel anxious and fearful anymore."

Five Effective Ways to Encourage Deep Play

1 ▶ PLAY WITH OTHERS

Playing with others is unifying. In their shared desire to keep the fun going, people playing together are more naturally cooperative and harmonious; their personal problems usually fade away into the background.

Go for a walk with a young child. Let the child set the tempo. As you enter fully into the child's world, observe how your own world changes.

Walk with a puppy or any animal that will accompany you. Observe its natural curiosity and enthusiasm. The caretaker of a guest ranch in Wyoming told me the story of Chandler, a resident Canadian goose who had imprinted on a staff member: "One day four international bankers, clothed in cowboy attire, knocked on my door and asked, 'Can Chandler come out and play? We're going swimming in the lake.'"

Chandler—like all geese—loved water, to play with him at the lake was delightful.

2 ▶ MOVE AND CHALLENGE YOURSELF

Physical movement shifts awareness from mind to body; it calms habitual over-thinking, the greatest hindrance to the spirit of play. Challenge yourself with a demanding task, such as navigating a starlit trail at night without using artificial light. As you feel your way forward, your mind will no longer coast along on automatic; your sensory and kinesthetic faculties will be on full alert.

3 ▶ CREATE FRESHNESS AND IMMEDIACY

As people age, they too often become "psychological antiques": creatures of habit, comfortable with things as they are. Human "antiques" have lost the spirit of adventure.

Strengthened by repeated behavior, existing neural pathways reduce the intensity of our direct perception by masking current experience. Instead of *seeing* the colorful bird before us, we *recall* a memory of a bird, or *think* of what we already know about the bird. The mind, categorizing present as past, perceives things secondhand, and thereby diminishes our sense of awe and connection with the natural world.

Learning something new or changing one's perspective can bring intense focus to the present moment; this state of heightened alertness will override the mind's tendency to categorize the present as the past. The physical senses, now fully engaged, mirror a more vivid world. "If we could see the miracle of a single flower clearly," Jack Kornfield wrote, "our whole life would change."

Sharing Nature activities sharpen awareness by asking players to perform simple tasks such as sketching their favorite scene, counting the different shades of green in a meadow, or recording how the natural world changes at sundown. Sunset viewers, for example, take note of clouds turning color, bats beginning to fly, the first star appearing, and wind speed or direction shifting.

Many Sharing Nature activities use change of perspective to create a feeling of newness. In *Micro-Hike*, children go on a very small "hike" by following a piece of string three to five feet long. They crawl on their belly or on their hands and knees and, through a magnifying glass, observe the tiny, fascinating world beneath them.

Breaking away from established routine opens our spirit to experience nature in fresh ways. Many of my most memorable nature outings have come when I was out before dawn to witness night transitioning to day.

Learning a new skill—dancing, singing, or speaking a foreign language—awakens a strong sense of immediacy and freshness.

4 ▶ FOCUS YOUR PLAY ON THE ACTUAL EXPERIENCE

Legendary UCLA basketball coach John Wooden won ten NCAA national championships in twelve years, a historically successful period that included a run of eighty-eight wins in a row. What was his secret? One player remembered "Coach Wooden didn't talk about winning—ever." The coach's guidance, as recalled by another player, Fred Slaughter, was invariably to focus on the actual experience:

There were four or five games in my career at UCLA when we started out behind something like 18-2—just getting killed. I'd look over at Coach Wooden, and there he'd sit on the bench with his program rolled up in his hand—totally unaffected, almost like we were ahead. And I'd think to myself, "Hey, if he's not worried why should I be worried? Let's just do what the guy told us to do."

And you know what? We won all those games except one, and even that was close.[36]

What did Coach Wooden tell his players?

> "Forget about the scoreboard, the standings, and what might happen in the future, and just focus on doing [your] jobs to the best of your ability.... keep your eye on the ball, not ... somewhere out in the distant future.... Long-term success requires short-term focus."[37]

"Play with the highest intensity," Wooden told his players. Play demands engagement; the greater the focus and intensity, the richer the play experience and learning.

5 ▶ CULTIVATE A SENSE OF ALIVENESS

That which is needed for deep play is equally necessary for meditation practice: childlike openness and inner freedom. Meditation—one-pointed concentration leading to absorption—can free us from the inner blocks to deep play. By calming the thinking mind, meditation instills in the meditator play's core qualities: freedom from self-consciousness and expansion of awareness.

Those who meditate regularly cultivate within themselves the attributes of deep play. They respond to life with originality, authenticity, courage, oneness of purpose, and a marvelous sense of wholeness.*

---

* For a simple, easy-to-learn yet powerful meditation technique, see the appendix.

Share the Spirit of Deep Play

Scientists know today that forests behave like cooperative communities: Individual trees share resources with one another and thus help the whole forest thrive. Even feeble trees—sustained by stronger trees—are essential to woodland vitality; they keep the canopy cover intact, thereby preventing hot sun and wind from heating the cool, moist air beneath the canopy.

Just as every woodland tree plays a crucial role in maintaining forest health, so each of us can play a beneficial role in life. Deep play, by uniting us with others and with nature, can prepare us to play our life roles with beauty and grace.

> Play can become a doorway to a new self, one much more in tune with the world. Because play [involves] trying on new behaviors and thoughts, it frees us from established patterns. . . . When we engage in fantasy play at any age, we bend the reality of our ordinary lives, and in the process germinate new ideas and ways of being.[38]

"The . . . source of knowledge," writes Albert Einstein, "is experience." Play, by inspiring the whole being, stimulates an exceptionally fruitful learning experience. If you instruct others—whether formally or informally—incorporating play into your classes can bring greater enthusiasm, retention, inner understanding, and uplifted consciousness to your students—and for you as teacher, a richer, more joyful experience.

We owe it to ourselves, to those we care for, and to all those we share this Earth with—to live more in the spirit and connectedness of deep play.

Chapter Fourteen

FOUR DEEP NATURE PLAY GAMES

1 ▶ CAMERA

Camera is one of the most powerful and memorable Sharing Nature games. In a simple way, it quiets distracting thoughts and restlessness so that one can see clearly.

Camera is played with two people: one person is the photographer and the other the camera. The photographer guides the camera, who has his eyes closed, on a search for beautiful and captivating pictures. When the photographer sees something he likes, he points the camera at it, to frame the object he wants to shoot.

The photographer signals the camera to open his lens (his eyes) by tapping twice on the camera's shoulder. Three seconds later, a third tap tells the camera to close his eyes again. For the first picture, it may help to say "Open" with the first two taps, and "Close" with the third.

Have the camera keep his eyes closed between pictures—to give the three-second "exposure" the impact of surprise. Encourage photographer and camera to walk in silence (speaking only if absolutely necessary) to enhance the camera's experience.

Participants have often told me that they've remembered the images of their photographs for longer than five years. In addition to the visual power of this exercise, the camera, during his periods of sightlessness, will also experience a magnification of his other senses.

After taking four to six photographs, the camera and the photographer trade roles.

Because the experience is so compelling, a beautiful rapport is established between the photographer and the human camera. It's heartwarming to observe grandparents and grandchildren, and other pairings, carefully guiding each other and delighting in the wondrous scenes of nature around them.

You can experience by yourself how *Camera* intensifies awareness. Select an area with varied terrain that's mostly clear of obstructions. Since you'll be walking alone, take along a hiking staff or pole for security and guidance.

Choose a safe route leading to interesting features such as large rocks, trees, or an arresting view. Close your eyes and begin walking. Notice how your leg muscles compensate for the unevenness of the terrain. Feel the warmth of the sun and the wind blowing against your body, and listen to the insects singing and buzzing close by.

As you walk, you can (as needed to stay on course) open your eyes just enough to detect blurry shapes.

When you sense that you're near something intriguing, open your eyes to take its picture. Opening your eyes for only the suggested three seconds keeps the attention sharply focused on the subject the whole time. When the exposures are longer, the mind tends to wander.

Continue to tread carefully while taking a few more photographs.

MORE CAMERA TIPS:

- Sensitively guide the camera by holding his hand and gently pulling his arm in the direction you want to go. Go slowly, and remain watchful for obstacles on the ground and for low-lying tree branches.

- Make the photographs stunning by taking shots from unusual angles and perspectives. For example, you can lie down under a tree and take your picture looking upward, or you can put your camera very close to a tree's bark or leaves.

- You can prepare the camera's vision for the next picture by telling him which lens to use. For a picture of a flower, tell the camera to choose a close-up lens; for a sweeping scenic panorama, a wide-angle lens; and for a faraway object, a telephoto lens.

- Photographers can also pan the camera—i.e., move it slowly with the shutter held open, like a movie camera. While panning, you can keep the shutter open longer, since the movement will hold the camera's interest. You can also pan vertically—for example, start at the base of a tree and slowly move up the trunk to the highest branches.

- After participants have played both roles, each player can "develop" (sketch from memory) one of the pictures he took while he was the camera. Then have each camera give his developed picture to the photographer.

- Children younger than twelve normally should pair with an adult or a mature teenager. Younger children don't have enough awareness of others to allow them to guide another child. It is, however, fine to have a young child lead a parent or grandparent. In this situation, I recommend letting the adult camera know it's okay to peek from time to time.

- Make sure to tell players about any potential dangers such as poisonous plants, harmful insect nests, or animal holes.

From *Sharing Nature: Nature Awareness Activities for All Ages*

2 ▶ SOUND MAP

The drumming of a woodpecker—wind streaming through the trees—flutelike calls of a hermit thrush—water cascading down a steep, rocky incline.

Enchanting choruses of natural sounds delight players of *Sound Map*. Children love this activity and sit surprisingly still while mapping the sounds around them.

To play, give each person a piece of paper with an X marked in the center. Tell the participants that the paper is a sound map and that the X represents where each player is sitting (once he's chosen his spot). When a player hears a sound, he makes a mark on the paper to represent the sound. The location of the mark should indicate the direction and distance of the sound from the player's seat. Tell players not to draw a detailed picture for each sound, but to make just a simple mark. For example, a few wavy lines could represent a gust of wind, or a musical note could indicate a singing bird. Making simple marks keeps the focus on listening rather than on drawing.

Encourage the players to close their eyes while listening for sounds. To help them increase their hearing ability, ask them to make "fox" ears by cupping their hands behind the ears. This hand position will create a greater surface area to capture sounds. To hear a variety of natural sounds, choose an area that encompasses several habitats, such as meadow, stream, and forest.

How long should you play? From 4 to 10 minutes is good—depending on the player's age and interest level, and on how active the animals are.

Sitting quietly—listening to the soothing voices of nearby trees, birds, and rustling grasses—calms us and deepens our appreciation for the life around us. *Sound Map* is an excellent activity for instilling greater awareness of one's surroundings.

"This earth was the most glorious musical instrument, and I was audience to its strains." —*Thoreau*

From *Sharing Nature: Nature Awareness Activities for All Ages*

I n this activity, you choose a rock, a plant, an animal, or a natural feature that has an interesting story to tell. For example, you can pick a dragonfly, a yellow flower, a boulder, a mountain peak, or even the wind.

Get to know your choice as well as you can. Try to learn about it in as many different ways as possible. For example, if you choose a rock or plant, you can feel its texture with your hands. See if anything grows on it. Look for evidence that something—such as fire, drought, or erosion—might have harmed or affected it in some way. Stand a short distance away and see how it fits into and interacts with its surroundings.

Imagine what its life might be like, and tell what you admire about it. Think also about the kinds of life experiences it might have had. Geologists have said that some rocks in the Grand Canyon are two billion years old. It's fun to think of all the things that have happened to those rocks since their creation. Mountain ranges have risen and fallen, deserts have come and gone, and seas have arrived and departed. Dinosaurs, mammoths, and camels have all in their turns walked the land.

While interviewing your subject and writing answers to your questions, try to see life from its point of view. Because your rock, plant, or animal cannot talk to you in the human sense, use your imagination to come up with the answers; if you like, you can try listening quietly for thoughts that tell you how your friend might respond.

Wild animals and plants attract us because we have a natural affinity for those sharing the gift of life. Humanizing nature helps us feel to some degree that all beings are like us.

HOW TO PLAY:

Select the category that matches your subject, then ask and answer the questions that most apply. Feel free to make up your own questions and conversations. Adults with young children can read the questions aloud and write down their children's answers.

ROCK, NATURAL FEATURE, OR PLANT

- How old are you?
- Where did you come from?
- Have you always been the size you are now?
- What is it like living in this particular place?
- What events have you seen in your life?
- Who comes to visit you?
- How do you benefit others?
- How do they help you?
- Is there something special you would like to tell me?

ANIMAL

Look for an animal that's easy to observe. It might be an insect, lizard, or ground squirrel. Imagine yourself becoming the animal. Try not to disturb or frighten it. Ask and answer some of the questions below:

- What are you doing now?
- Where do you live?
- What do you eat, and how do you find your food?
- How does your life benefit others?
- How do they help you?
- What are the things you like most about your life?
- Do you ever travel to other places?
- What would you like to tell others about yourself?

Take at least ten minutes for your interview and note the responses you feel.

From *Sharing Nature: Nature Awareness Activities for All Ages*

4 ▶ VERTICAL POEM

Because of its contemplative and sharing component, *Vertical Poem* is both an inspirational and a bonding activity. To practice this exercise, first observe something that captivates you—perhaps a field of flowers or a secluded sea cove. Notice its effect on you, and choose a word that captures your feeling. Then use each letter of the word to begin a line of your poem.

The simple structure for a vertical poem makes it very easy to write. After successfully crafting their verses, people have exclaimed to me, "It's been forty years since I've written a poem!"

Composing a vertical poem quiets a small party of friends and allows them to become more present and immersed in their surroundings.

The Vertical Poem below was written in
a forest in Northern California:

Fragrances of oak and pine

Open up the heart and mind.

Remain still awhile and listen:

Everywhere is Nature's song—

Sometimes as silent as a leaf falling;

Time is suspended.

—Tom W.

TO PRACTICE VERTICAL POEM

Write the word you've chosen, one letter on each line. Then use each letter to begin a line of your poem.

_____   _____

_____   _____

_____   _____

_____   _____

_____   _____

_____   _____

_____   _____

_____   _____

_____   _____

_____   _____

_____   _____

_____   _____

_____   _____

From The Sky and Earth Touched Me

APPENDIX

MEDITATION: WATCHING THE BREATH

Preparation

One of the best ways to relax the body is first to tense it. Then, as you relax, you will find a release of tensions you didn't even know existed. Begin your meditation experience by practicing the following two relaxation techniques. The first exercise relaxes your body, and the second calms your mind.

1. Inhale and tense the whole body, then throw the breath out and relax. Repeat this exercise three times to help rid your body of unconscious tensions.

2. The breath reflects one's mental state. As the breath becomes calmer, so does the mind, and vice versa. Before you meditate, relax by doing this simple breathing exercise:

> Inhale slowly counting one to four, hold your breath to the same count, then exhale to an equal count. This breath cycle is one round of "even-count breathing."

> You may either increase or decrease the number of counts to find your most comfortable rhythm, but keep the length of inhalation, retention, and exhalation equal. Practice "even-count breathing" six times.

Meditation

As the breath becomes calmer and more refined during meditation, you may experience a joyous feeling of peace. Practice the following meditation technique to help calm your breath, your mind, and your whole being:

Inhale deeply, then slowly exhale. Wait for the breath to come in of its own accord, and watch its inflow. As the breath flows out naturally, again observe the movement. Don't inhale and exhale deliberately; instead simply be an observer.

Notice and feel the movement of breath on the inside of your nose, with your attention on the breath itself, not on the nose.

Be particularly aware of the rest points between the breaths. Enjoy the peace, and the feeling of inward release and freedom that you feel when your body is without breath.

Practice for ten minutes if you can. When you finish observing your breath, continue to sit quietly and enjoy the stillness and serenity you feel.

NOTES

CHAPTER 2

1. Dee Joy Coulter, Ed.D., *Original Mind* (Boulder, CO: Sounds True, 2014), 12.
2. Richard St. Barbe Baker, *My Life My Trees* (Forres, Scotland: Findhorn Publications, 1979), 10–11.
3. Michael Mendizza with Joseph Chilton Pearce, *Magical Parent Magical Child* (Berkeley, CA: North Atlantic Books, 2003, 2004), ix.

CHAPTER 3

4. Michael Mendizza with Joseph Chilton Pearce, *Magical Parent Magical Child* (Berkeley, CA: North Atlantic Books, 2003, 2004), 28, 27.

CHAPTER 4

5. Carla Hannaford, Ph.D., *Smart Moves* (Salt Lake City, UT: Great River Books, 1995, 2005),15, 69.
6. Ibid, 69.
7. Brain HQ, *What Is Brain Plasticity?* (Posit Science, 2016, http://www.brainhq.com/brain-resources/brain-plasticity/what-is-brain-plasticity.) (Accessed July 15, 2016.)

CHAPTER 5

8. Marc Bekoff, Ph.D., *The Emotional Lives of Animals* (Novato, CA: New World Library, 2007), 97, 96.
9. Marc Bekoff, Ph.D., *Minding Animals: Awareness, Emotions, and Heart* (New York, NY: Oxford University Press, 2002), 126.
10. Nick Jans, *A Wolf Called Romeo* (New York, NY: Mariner Books, 2014), 64-65.

CHAPTER 7

11. Stuart Brown, M.D., *Play* (New York, NY: Avery , 2010), 37.
12. Peter Gray, Ph.D., *Free to Learn* (New York, NY: Basic Books, 2013), 146,148.

13. Lev Vygotsky, *Mind in Society* (Cambridge, MA: Harvard University Press, 1978), 95.

14. Lev Vygotsky (1978). The Role of Play in Development (pp. 92–94). In *Mind in Society*. (Trans. M. Cole). (Cambridge, MA: Harvard University Press), 6. www.colorado.edu/physics/EducationIssues/T&Lphys/PDFs/vygot_chap7.pdf. (Accessed May 14, 2017.)

15. Lev Vygotsky, *Mind in Society* (Cambridge, MA: Harvard University Press, 1978), 94–95.

CHAPTER 8

16. Dr. Mike Bechtle, *Why Kids Are Creative, and How They Lose It as Adults* (http://www.mikebechtle.com/why-kids-are-creative-and-how-they-lose-it-as-adults). (Accessed March 21, 2016.)

17. Dee Joy Coulter, Ed.D., *Original Mind* (Boulder, CO: Sounds True, 2014), 2.

18. Ibid, 3.

19. Evelyn Fox Keller, *A Feeling for the Organism* (San Francisco, CA: W.H. Freeman & Co, 1983), 117.

CHAPTER 9

20. Matthew A. Killingsworth and Daniel T. Gilbert, *Science* 330 (November 12, 2010). (Accessed online May 1, 2013.)

CHAPTER 10

21. Joseph Cornell, *John Muir: My Life with Nature* (Nevada City: Dawn Publications, 2000), 59.

22. Sir Francis Younghusband, *The Heart of Nature* (New York, NY: E.P. Dutton and Company, 1922), 168.

CHAPTER 11

23. Richard Feynman, *Surely You're Joking, Mr. Feynman* (New York, NY: W. W. Norton & Company, 1985), 199-201.

24. Michael Michalko, *Cracking Creativity: The Secrets of Creative Genius* (Berkeley, CA: Ten Speed Press, 1998), 209, 4.

25. Stuart Brown, M.D., *Play* (New York, NY: Avery, 2010), 60.

26. Adapted from a personal interview with Peter Jacobsen, Michael Mendizza with Joseph Chilton Pearce, *Magical Parent Magical Child* (Berkeley, CA: North Atlantic Books, 2003, 2004), 86.

27. Mark R. Lepper, David Greene, Richard E. Nisbett, "Undermining

Children's Intrinsic Interest with Extrinsic Reward: A Test of the 'Over-justification' Hypothesis," *Journal of Personality and Social Psychology*, 28, 1 (October 1973): 129-137. (Accessed online September 10, 2016.)

CHAPTER 12

28. Johnny Miller, *Golf.Com Magazine* interview. (Originally appeared March 1982.) (Accessed October 12, 2016.)
29. Michael Mendizza with Joseph Chilton Pearce, *Magical Parent Magical Child* (Berkeley, CA: North Atlantic Books, 2003, 2004), 5.
30. John Muir, *John of the Mountains*, ed. Linnie Marsh Wolfe (Madison, Wisconsin: University of Wisconsin Press, 1979), 296.
31. Frederick Reimers, *It's Time for Doctors to Prescribe Outdoor Therapy* (Santa Fe, NM: Outsideonline.com, *Outside Magazine*, October 24, 2016). (Accessed November 2, 2016.)

CHAPTER 13

32. Nat Nanton, *How to Have Fun Like Children: 15 Joyful Tips* (Tiny Buddha: http://tinybuddha.com/blog/how-to-have-fun-like-children-15-joyful-tips). (Accessed September 15, 2016.)
33. Peter Matthiessen, *The Snow Leopard* (New York, NY: Penguin Books, 1996), 41.
34. Maria Coffey, *Explorers of the Infinite* (New York, NY: Jeremy P. Tarcher/Penguin, 2008), 55.
35. Ibid, 56.
36. John Wooden and Steve Jamison, *Wooden on Leadership* (New York, NY: McGraw-Hill Books, 2005), 217, 115.
37. Ibid, 211, 216.
38. Stuart Brown, M.D., *Play*, (New York, NY: Avery, 2010), 92, 93.

PHOTOGRAPHER CREDITS

ANANDA VILLAGE

oseph Bharat Cornell and his wife, Anandi, are residents of Ananda Village, a 700-acre cooperative community located in the Sierra Foothills of Northern California. Based on the principles of simple living and high thinking, Ananda is one of the most successful intentional communities in the world. Through its retreat centers, Living Wisdom Schools, beautiful gardens, organic farming, publications, online classes, and example of living in harmony with nature and with one another, Ananda serves visitors from all over the world. Founded in 1969 by Swami Kriyananda, Ananda practices the universal teachings of Paramhansa Yogananda.

For more information: anandavillage.org

Sharing Nature®
WORLDWIDE

THE NATURE AWARENESS WORK

of Joseph Bharat Cornell

Joseph Cornell is an internationally renowned author and founder of Sharing Nature Worldwide, one of the planet's most widely respected nature awareness programs. His first book, *Sharing Nature with Children*, "sparked a worldwide revolution in nature education" and has been published in twenty languages and sold half a million copies. He is the honorary president of Sharing Nature Association of Japan, which has 10,000 members and 35,000 trained leaders.

He the author of the Sharing Nature Book Series, used by millions of parents, educators, naturalists, and youth and religious leaders all over the world. Mr. Cornell's books, *Listening to Nature* and *The Sky and Earth Touched Me*, have inspired thousands of adults to deepen their relationship with nature. Two recent books of his: *The Sky and Earth Touched Me* and *Sharing Nature* were awarded Indie Book Grand Prize Winners for Non-Fiction.

The U.S. Fish & Wildlife Service selected Mr. Cornell's *Sharing Nature with Children* as one of the fifteen most influential books published since 1890 for connecting children and families to nature. His highly effective outdoor learning strategy, Flow Learning™, was featured by the U.S. National Park Service as one of five recommended learning theories, along with the works of Maria Montessori, Howard Gardner, John Dewey, and Jean Piaget.

Mr. Cornell has received many international awards for his Sharing Nature books and work. He received the prestigious Countess Sonja-Bernadotte Prize in Germany for his vast influence on environmental education in Central Europe. In 2011 Cornell was selected as one of the world's "100 most influential opinion leaders committed to the Environment" by the French organization, Les Anges Gardiens de la Planète.

Known for his warmth and joyful enthusiasm, Cornell "has a genius for finding the essence of a subject, explaining it in clear and compelling ways, and then giving the reader creative exercises to gain an actual experience."

For more information about Joseph Cornell's books and activities visit: **www.jcornell.org**

SHARING NATURE
WELLNESS PROGRAM

John Muir said, "Nature's peace flows into us as sunshine flows into trees." Nature, the great healer, offers gifts of joyful serenity and vitality to every receptive heart.

During a Sharing Nature Wellness program you'll practice nature exercises to quiet your mind and open your heart to all creation. You will learn how to internalize your experience of nature and feel more at peace with life.

You'll delight in joyful nature awareness activities, feel more positive and affirmative, and enjoy a spirit of community and communion with others and with nature. Nature's benevolent presence will remind you of life's higher priorities.

SHARING THE JOY OF NATURE SINCE 1979

Sharing Nature is a worldwide movement dedicated to helping children and adults deepen their relationship with nature. We offer training workshops, keynote presentations, online resources, webinars, and books to help people feel closer to nature and to others. Our Wellness programs provide uplifting experiences and healing for individuals, and for leaders in business, education, religion, and the public sector.

Sharing Nature coordinators are represented in numerous countries around the world and would be happy to speak to your group or organization. Our coordinators are exceptional individuals who love nature and people, and can bring them beautifully together.

We would love to hear from you. Please contact us to learn more about our offerings around the world.

Sharing Nature Worldwide

14618 Tyler Foote Road   Phone: (530) 478-7650
Nevada City, CA 95959   info@sharingnature.com

OTHER BOOKS BY JOSEPH CORNELL
Published by Crystal Clarity

SHARING NATURE
Nature Awareness Activities for All Ages

The book that sparked a worldwide revolution in nature education, *Sharing Nature* makes experiencing nature fun. An extraordinary treasure trove of games and activities that tap into our natural curiosity, imagination, and wonder that takes readers beyond their intellects and into their hearts, where true understanding and appreciation take place.

Cornell's unique blend of knowledge and warmth creates a contagious atmosphere for learning, with over 250 photos and comprehensive easy-to-follow instructions for all the nature games.

THE SKY AND EARTH TOUCHED ME
Sharing Nature® Wellness Exercises

Written for adults desiring a deeper connection with nature, this book takes the Sharing Nature exercises to a higher level, and offers a transformative guide for healing and well-being in nature.

There is a tremendous power in these activities. One moment of touching nature can inspire you for a lifetime. Practicing these simple exercises will immerse you in the natural world and open your heart to all creation.

"Enriching, awakening, and life-changing nature experiences."

—Roderic Knowles, Founder of Living Tree
Educational Foundation, author of *Gospel of the Living Tree*

LISTENING TO NATURE
How to Deepen Your Awareness of Nature

The beloved and bestselling book *Listening to Nature* will open your eyes and your heart to the peace and joyous spirit of the natural world. Joseph Bharat Cornell offers adults a sensitive and lively guide to deeper awareness of nature. Cornell's innovative nature awareness techniques combine with stunning photographs and quotations from famous naturalists to enliven your experience of nature. This new edition has been extensively rewritten and includes dozens of new photographs and quotations.

"A splendid masterpiece that captures the 'Oneness' we are all seeking to achieve with Nature."

—Tom Brown, Jr., author of *The Tracker*

AUM: THE MELODY OF LOVE

AUM is God's tangible presence in creation. By hearing the Cosmic Sound, conscious contact with Spirit is established. Saint Francis described celestial AUM as "music so sweet and beautiful that, had it lasted a moment longer, I would have melted away from the sheer joy of it."

AUM is vibrating blissfully in every atom in the universe; when one listens to it, he enters into the stream of God's love. Communion with AUM expands one's consciousness and unites him with Spirit.

"Cornell invites us, through AUM, into the very source of nature, the fount of universal religious experience, and the essential experience of self. This intriguing book could very well change the way you see everything."

—Garth Gilchrist, nature writer, storyteller, portrayer of John Muir

Crystal Clarity Publishers offers a great number of additional resources to assist you on your life journey, including many other books, and a wide variety of inspirational and relaxation music and videos. To find out more information, please contact us at:

www.crystalclarity.com

14618 Tyler Foote Road / Nevada City, CA 95959
TOLL FREE 800.424.1055 or 530.478.7600
FAX: 530.478.7610
EMAIL: clarity@crystalclarity.com

 PLAY!